A WORLD OF DISCOVERY

JAMES BROWN & RICHARD PLATT

CANDLEWICK STUDIO

CONTENTS

THE WHEEL

*Wheels seem so essential that we can't imagine life without them—
or conceive of any invention that might be more clever or more useful.*

W E DON'T KNOW who invented the wheel, but we do know where they probably did it. The earliest words to describe wheels, carts, and their parts are in the language that was spoken in what is now Ukraine, around 3500 BCE. That seems like a long time ago, but by then we already had weaving, sailing ships, mirrors, and makeup. So why did it take so long to invent the wheel? Because it's difficult. Making a wheel circular isn't the only challenge. You also need an axle that is round and straight, and a hole in the exact center of the wheel. This must be *slightly* bigger than the axle. If you get anything wrong, your wheel won't turn—or will soon wear out.

GOING "POTTY"
The very first wheels did not roll on roads; they spun pots in perfect circles. Fast-spinning potters' wheels were in use in Mesopotamia 5,000 years ago, long before wheeled vehicles took to the road.

FIRST WHEELS

The earliest practical wheels were made from planks joined edge to edge and cut in circles. The development of lightweight spoked wheels, around 2000 BCE in Asia Minor, was a military breakthrough. It made possible fast-moving chariots that could carry a driver and archers. Chariot warfare was at its most intense in the thirteenth century BCE: at the Battle of Kadesh in northern Syria as many as 5,000 chariots wheeled around the battlefield as the local Hittite people clashed with Egyptian invaders.

BURY ME WITH MY WHEELS
Gearheads didn't invent wheel worship. From 2000 BCE, powerful, wealthy people were buried with their means of transport. These chariot burials have been found all over Europe as well as in China.

SPEEDING THINGS UP

Making wheels spin faster required two companion inventions: roads and tires. From the eighteenth century on, rutted mud tracks were surfaced with stone, speeding traffic along. Inflatable rubber tires, introduced in the 1880s by Scottish inventor John Dunlop, gave newly invented motor cars a better grip and a smoother ride. Rimmed with rubber and matched with a ribbon of tar, the wheel zipped us into the highway age.

SIDEWALK SURFING

Advanced technology transformed street sports just as it did road transportation. Skateboarding was an obscure Californian craze until, in the early 1970s, durable polyurethane replaced the metal or ceramic wheels that had been in use since the boards were invented nearly 30 years before. The wheels' speed and grip enabled the stunts that define the modern sport.

LET'S TARMACADAM IT!
The ancient Romans built fine roads all over Europe, but these crumbled when their empire collapsed around 400 CE. Fourteen centuries later, Scottish engineer John McAdam reinvented the road, draining it with ditches and paving it with layers of crushed, rolled stones. These "McAdamized" roads stood up to years of wear by iron-rimmed wheels. Welsh inventor Edgar Purnell Hooley added tar to form "tarmacadam," later shortened to *tarmac*.

THE EVOLUTION OF THE WHEEL

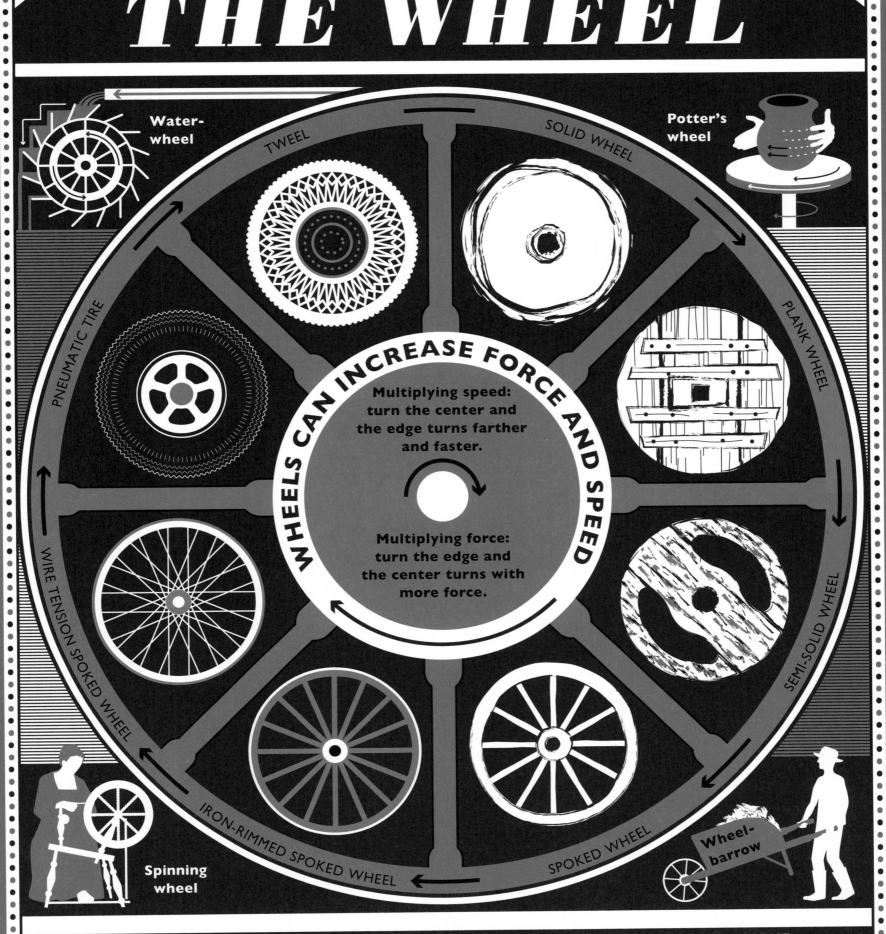

Water-wheel

Potter's wheel

TWEEL

SOLID WHEEL

PNEUMATIC TIRE

PLANK WHEEL

WHEELS CAN INCREASE FORCE AND SPEED

Multiplying speed: turn the center and the edge turns farther and faster.

Multiplying force: turn the edge and the center turns with more force.

WIRE TENSION SPOKED WHEEL

SEMI-SOLID WHEEL

Spinning wheel

IRON-RIMMED SPOKED WHEEL

SPOKED WHEEL

Wheel-barrow

WHEELS REDUCE THE FORCE OF FRICTION AND SO MAKE THINGS EASIER TO MOVE

Applied force

Gravitational force

Frictional force

Friction between the object and the ground makes it difficult to push the object.

Friction gives the wheels grip on the road.

Gravitational force

Applied force

Less friction between the wheels and the axle makes it easier to push the object.

FIRE

By harnessing the searing power of dancing, flickering flames, our ancestors hugely improved their diet. Better food gave our ancestors better brains — and made us the humans we are today.

WHEN DID PEOPLE first learn to control fire? Evidence for the kindling of fire is uncertain, but the first people to tame it probably lived some 1.5 million years ago on the shores of Lake Turkana in what is now Kenya. These people most likely learned of fire's advantages from lightning-strike blazes. Full control of fire, however, meant making flames on demand. This may have come much, much later — there is no solid proof until 13,000 years ago, in Europe.

THE PROMETHEUS MYTH

There are countless myths about fire's origins. In the ancient Greek myth, the Titan Prometheus stole fire from Zeus, the king of the gods, and gave it to humans. To punish him, Zeus chained Prometheus to a rock and commanded an eagle to peck at his liver for eternity.

LIGHTING THE BBQ

The ability to deliberately create and nurture flames was life-changing for early humans. And the greatest improvement was in cooking. Heat transforms food, making it more digestible and killing germs that could make a meal the diner's last. Anthropologists view the discovery of cooking as a major step in human evolution. Better food led to brainier, more successful humans.

Fire helped early people in other ways, too. Flames warmed our ancestors, allowing them to populate colder regions of the world. Fires kept predators at bay, they burned tracks through dense undergrowth, and they cleared land for farming.

> ### YOU CAN'T CALL 'EM THAT!
> John Walker first sold his matches as "Sulphurata Hyper-Oxygenata Fricts," but he quickly came up with a snappier name: Friction Lights. Nevertheless, he still sold only a few boxes a week.

FIRE-STARTING

The caveman image of rubbing two sticks together to make fire is not too far off, but this is not the only way to start a blaze. Bashing flint against "fool's gold" — iron pyrite — strikes sparks that ignite tinder (shreds of dry, flammable material), and even squeezing air in a bamboo tube can make enough heat

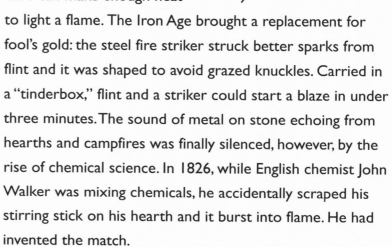

to light a flame. The Iron Age brought a replacement for fool's gold: the steel fire striker struck better sparks from flint and it was shaped to avoid grazed knuckles. Carried in a "tinderbox," flint and a striker could start a blaze in under three minutes. The sound of metal on stone echoing from hearths and campfires was finally silenced, however, by the rise of chemical science. In 1826, while English chemist John Walker was mixing chemicals, he accidentally scraped his stirring stick on his hearth and it burst into flame. He had invented the match.

Though fire played a major role in our evolution and exploration of the world, we no longer rely on naked flames as we once did. Nevertheless, fire still fascinates us, and it is central to religion and ritual. And what could ever replace the pleasure of crackling logs in a hearth or a candle on the dinner table?

> **"In order to find early fire, we have to work really, really hard."**
>
> **MICHAEL CHAZAN, DIRECTOR OF THE ARCHAEOLOGY CENTRE AT THE UNIVERSITY OF TORONTO, IN 2017**

THE FIRE TRIANGLE

TO KINDLE A FIRE, IT IS NECESSARY TO SUPPLY ONLY THREE THINGS. TO EXTINGUISH IT, JUST REMOVE ONE OF THEM.

FIRE NEEDS THREE ELEMENTS TO START

OXYGEN

Air is about one-fifth oxygen — and provides enough of the gas to support the burning of most solid fuels.

HEAT

Energy from the sun, from friction, or from electricity or a chemical reaction can raise the temperature high enough to start a fire.

FUEL

Fuel can take many forms: it can be a gas, a liquid, or a solid.

THE SCIENCE OF
FIRE & FLAMES

A CANDLE FLAME TYPICALLY BURNS AT AROUND 1,800 DEGREES FAHRENHEIT (1,000 DEGREES CELSIUS).

FLAMES ALWAYS POINT UP
Gravity gives candle flames their familiar form. Heat from the burning wax fuel warms the air around the flame, making it lighter. The warm air rises, sucking the flame into a teardrop shape. In the microgravity of space, flames are circular.

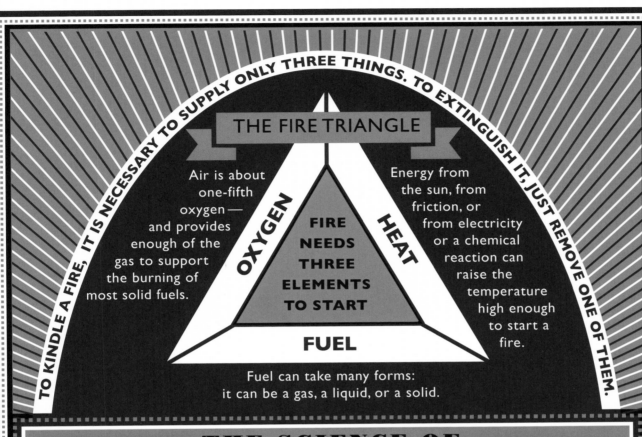

HOT AIR

COOL AIR

OUTER ZONE
The hottest part is dark, as fuel is burning efficiently and completely.

MIDDLE ZONE
Here is cooler. Carbon particles glow brightly as they are partially burned.

INNER ZONE
Lack of oxygen means there is little burning here.

TIME

Powered by swinging pendulums, accurate clocks changed the way we live. Able to keep time down to the minute, we let a ticking machine set the pace of our day.

SITTING IN PISA CATHEDRAL in 1581, a medical student was distracted from the service by a swinging lamp that a church official had pulled aside to light the candles. The lamp swung in a wide arc, which gradually settled to a gentle sway. The student noticed that each swing, however wide, took nearly the same time, and he later realized that the regular movement would be a handy way to measure time. In sixteenth-century Italy, measuring time precisely wasn't practical. Although mechanical clocks existed, they gained or lost at least 15 minutes a day, and consequently had only an hour hand.

LONG-FORGOTTEN PENDULUM

The student distracted from his prayers was scientific genius Galileo Galilei, who remembered the Pisa Cathedral lamp years later, at the age of seventy-seven. It inspired him to design a machine that kept time using a pendulum—a swinging, weighted rod. By now, Galileo was blind and in the last year of his life, so his son tried to build the clock, but without success. Around 1656, Dutch mathematician and scientist Christiaan Huygens had more luck. He managed to make a pendulum's regular swing control the clockwork by linking it to a rocking device called an escapement (see opposite). Huygens's clock kept time to within 10 seconds a day and was precise enough to make a minute hand useful. The pendulum was such an improvement that most clocks were modified to use them.

CHANGING THE WORLD

If time could be measured accurately, so too could work. Before clocks were reliable, workers were paid by the task or the day. Afterward, their work—and pay—was measured by the minute. Steam may have powered the Industrial Revolution, but it was the pendulum clock that regulated and ruled its workers.

CHURCH TIME
Until the invention of the pendulum clock, monks were the only people who really "watched the clock"—or, rather, listened to it. They prayed at regular intervals at least eight times a day, and at night the bell on a mechanical monastic alarum clock summoned them to the chapel.

Accurate clocks changed travel, too. Mariners used them to calculate how far they had traveled by checking the time of local noon—in other words, when the sun was at its highest. For every 17 miles (28 kilometers) they sailed west, noon was a minute later. This simple way of "finding longitude" gave sea captains a new confidence and has helped us map and explore our planet. In the latter half of the twentieth century, history repeated itself with the invention of satellite navigation (see page 53), which relies on super-precise clocks and can now lead travelers using GPS to within 16 feet of their destination.

GET A POTATO CLOCK
Huygens's invention of the balance spring in 1675 made pocket watches as accurate as clocks, and soon every wealthy person carried one—or two. Some joked that the second one was just a potato on a silver chain.

"The clocks at the factories ... were used ... for cheatery and oppression."
A NINETEENTH-CENTURY FACTORY WORKER COMPLAINS THAT HIS EMPLOYER ALTERS THE CLOCK TO LENGTHEN WORK HOURS

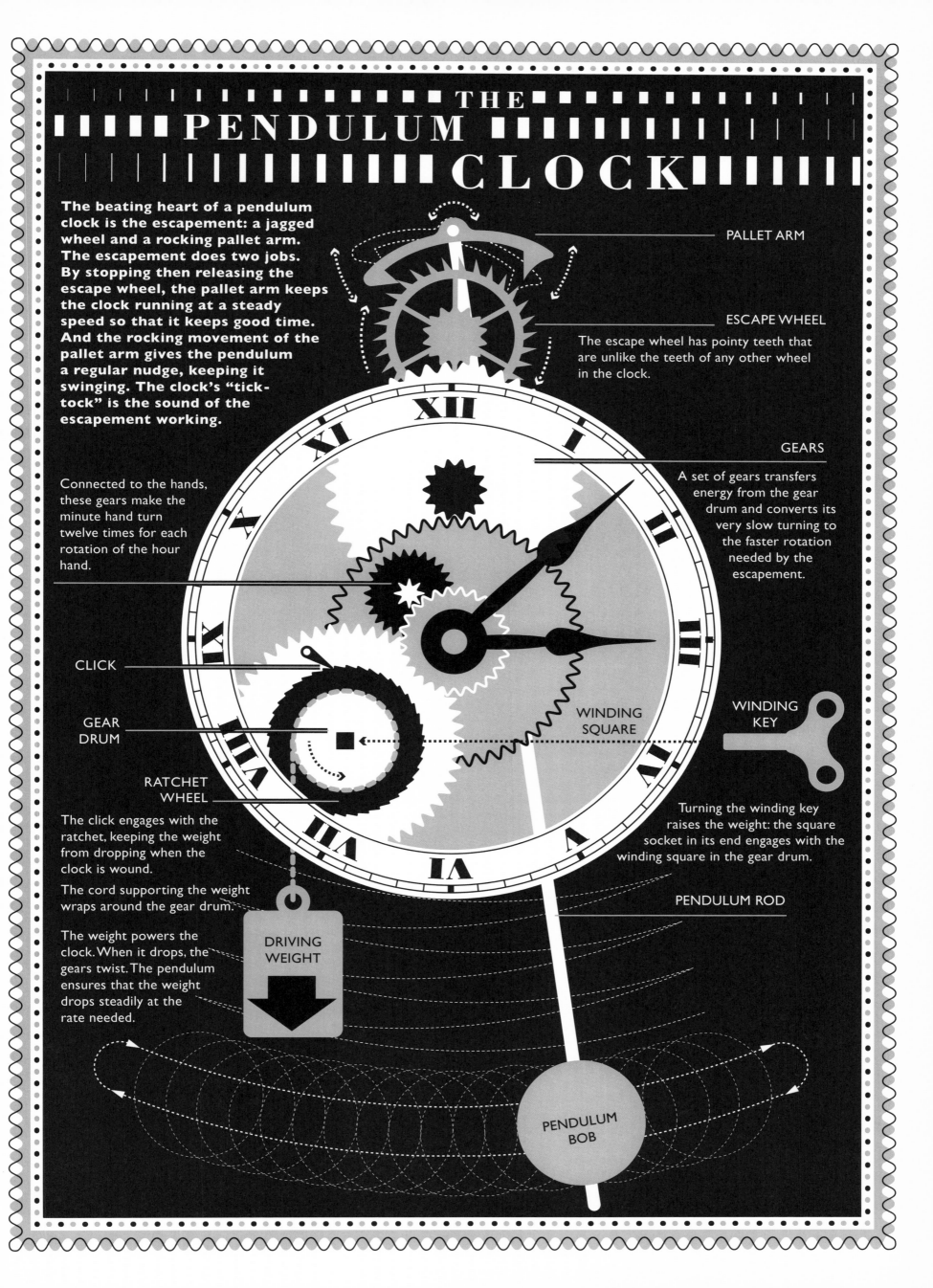

THE PENDULUM CLOCK

The beating heart of a pendulum clock is the escapement: a jagged wheel and a rocking pallet arm. The escapement does two jobs. By stopping then releasing the escape wheel, the pallet arm keeps the clock running at a steady speed so that it keeps good time. And the rocking movement of the pallet arm gives the pendulum a regular nudge, keeping it swinging. The clock's "tick-tock" is the sound of the escapement working.

PALLET ARM

ESCAPE WHEEL

The escape wheel has pointy teeth that are unlike the teeth of any other wheel in the clock.

GEARS

A set of gears transfers energy from the gear drum and converts its very slow turning to the faster rotation needed by the escapement.

Connected to the hands, these gears make the minute hand turn twelve times for each rotation of the hour hand.

CLICK

GEAR DRUM

RATCHET WHEEL

The click engages with the ratchet, keeping the weight from dropping when the clock is wound.

The cord supporting the weight wraps around the gear drum.

The weight powers the clock. When it drops, the gears twist. The pendulum ensures that the weight drops steadily at the rate needed.

WINDING SQUARE

WINDING KEY

Turning the winding key raises the weight: the square socket in its end engages with the winding square in the gear drum.

PENDULUM ROD

DRIVING WEIGHT

PENDULUM BOB

MONEY

In a simpler world, we wouldn't need money. We'd simply barter: swap things. But bartering doesn't work when the person who has what you want doesn't want what you're offering.

IN A FEW VERY isolated places in the world, there are still people who have no need for coins, bills, or credit cards. However, money is such a useful concept that it has become central to most of our lives. It is a very convenient way to store, measure, and exchange value. It hugely simplifies trade, particularly for services and for especially valuable items.

EARLY MONEY

Money began around 5,000 years ago with the exchange of useful items that had a value on which everyone agreed, such as cattle, metal objects, or measures of grain. Cowries—small seashells prized as jewelry—were widely used for money all over Africa and parts of Asia. But this commodity money was not as convenient as coins, which were small, standard, durable, and officially stamped with their value. Greek historian Herodotus credits the king of Lydia (now western Turkey) with the invention of gold and silver coins. Certainly Lydian coins minted around 700 BCE are the oldest archaeologists have found. But coins as currency did not catch on right away: for a long time after this, Indian people were using stamped metal bars as coins, and in China people paid with coins shaped like knives and spades.

The Chinese adopted round coins some 2,400 years ago, but by the eleventh century they had found an even better way to pay or save: banknotes. Originally devised as written receipts for coins in safe storage, banknotes soon became money in their own right. They were printed by the government and trusted as much as coins by the people who exchanged them in payment.

HEAVY MONEY

On the Pacific island of Yap, the traditional coins are *rai:* stone disks, some as big as 11 feet (3.6 meters) across and too big to move. To pay for something, a buyer doesn't move a big *rai* but agrees that it now belongs to the seller. When *rai* is being valued, size isn't the only factor: a small, well-made stone formerly owned by a great person is worth more than a larger, plain stone with no history.

VIRTUALLY INVISIBLE

Today, bank transfers, credit card payments, and other forms of electronic money are rapidly making coins and dollar bills look old-fashioned. Foreign travel has made us comfortable with changing money into many different currencies (see opposite), and online payments are as familiar as yesterday's pocket money. Numbers on a screen represent our wealth—just as the numbers on a banknote once represented the weight of gold for which it could be exchanged. What hasn't changed is that it is still trust that makes money work. We wouldn't click "buy now" if we thought the seller was dishonest or if we didn't trust the bank to pass on our payment. And then we would be back to swapping goats for stone axes.

WORTHLESS MONEY

Money can become worth less—or worthless—when the government that prints it fails or is not trusted. After Germany's defeat in World War I, inflation soared, slashing the value of the mark (the German currency). In January 1923, bread cost 250 marks a loaf. Ten months later the price had risen to over 200,000,000,000 marks! Today, Venezuela faces similar problems, with prices doubling every two weeks.

> **Chinese banknotes from the Ming Dynasty warned forgers that their heads would be cut off and promised informers 17 pounds (8 kilograms) of silver.**

WORLD CURRENCIES

There are almost 180 official currencies in use around the world. These 20 are the most commonly traded.

PAPER

When paper reached Europe, it kick-started a revolution in printing and knowledge. But paper's long history began in China, and not with ink and writing.

WHEN WRITING BEGAN in China, scribes scraped their picture symbols on turtle shells, animal bones, and bamboo strips. Later, they used brushes to paint words onto silk sheets. According to Chinese legend, writing on paper began in 105 CE when Cai Lun, a Han Dynasty official, watched wasps layer wood fibers into a fragile nest. Imitating them, he made paper from rags, fishing nets, tree bark, and hemp plants.

What is more likely is that Cai Lun was the first to describe papermaking; the oldest paper ever found—in Inner Mongolia—was made two or three centuries before Cai Lun lived. And it was too soft for writing: the earliest papers were used for wrapping—and as tissues.

READING AND WRITING

Paper did not instantly replace the silk sheets that scribes had previously used to write on: silk was still in use in the sixth century. But by then, resourceful Chinese people were making paper into clothes, hats, kites, and even tea bags. The Chinese guarded the skills of papermaking jealously, but they could not stop them from spreading. When Arab and Chinese armies clashed at the Battle of Talas in 751, papermakers were said to be among those taken prisoner. Legend has it that their knowledge helped their Arab captors make paper at Samarkand and later Baghdad. The mills of this thriving city became so famous that a Greek word for paper was

bagdatixon. Over the next five centuries, paper dramatically changed the Arab world. Words on paper replaced speech as the main way of passing on knowledge and belief.

DON'T WASTE IT

Despite the rise of electronic media, we still use masses of paper. Each year, the average American uses around 700 pounds (320 kilograms).

PAPER JOURNEY

In Europe, paper replaced vellum, the stretched and smooth-scraped skins of calves. Muslim-ruled Spain introduced Europeans to paper: by the start of the thirteenth century there were mills in France, and other countries soon followed.

Originally a handicraft, papermaking slowly became an industry in Europe. From the thirteenth century, waterwheels powered heavy wooden hammers that pounded rags into a pulp of fluffy fibers. Turning pulp into sheets remained hard handwork until French papermaker Louis-Nicolas Robert patented machines to make long ribbons of paper in 1799. Today's papermaking machines may be bigger and faster, but they are essentially the same.

The impact of paper on our world is hard to overstate. Paper's success was a necessary part of the triumph of printing, and of the huge spread of knowledge it made possible. Would paper's invention have been as important had printing not followed? Ask a cow!

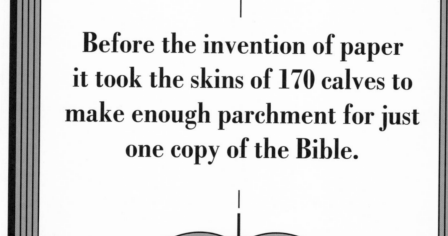

Before the invention of paper it took the skins of 170 calves to make enough parchment for just one copy of the Bible.

WIPE THAT!
Six hundred years before Europeans first wrote on paper, the Chinese were already wiping their backsides with it.

How is PAPER made?

1. Vast machines called tree harvesters cut forest trees. One tree can be enough to make about 8,000 sheets of paper.

2. Tumbling logs in a drum or cradle strips off the bark, which would otherwise spoil the paper.

3. Passing the logs through a chipper turns them into chips about the size of a small paper clip.

4. Cooking the wet chips in a digester like a giant pressure cooker softens them and bursts them apart into small wood fibers.

5. Sieving, washing, and bleaching creates pulp: watery, white fiber slush.

Waste paper can take the place of much of the wood fiber that goes into pulp, saving water, energy, and trees. However, pulp fibers get shorter every time paper is recycled, so most paper contains some pulp made from logs.

6. Pouring the pulp onto a moving mesh removes water, leaving a strip of fluffy paper.

7. In the press section of the paper machine, rollers squeeze out moisture.

8. Passing the paper strip through heated rollers dries it out. Coating sometimes follows for smoother, brighter paper.

9. Finally, paper is rolled on reels: it will be cut into sheets later.

EXPLOSIVES

*What began as a potion for eternal life swiftly became
"the devil's distillate"—a costly, dangerous dust that powered
guns and cannons, and created and destroyed empires.*

IN ANCIENT CHINA, religion, magic, and science came together in the laboratories of Taoist alchemists. In their search for spiritual purity and everlasting life, these experimenters purified yellow sulfur and white saltpeter powders.

Around 850 CE they mixed these two chemicals with powdered charcoal and made an explosive discovery. The potion they had created did not make them live forever, but it burned with a spectacular bang. They called it "fire potion"; we call it gunpowder, or black powder.

Gunpowder's first use was not for guns but for noisy entertainment. The Chinese traditionally drove off evil spirits by throwing bamboo into fire, where the tubular stems burst with loud explosions. The new powder made louder, brighter bangs. However, its military value was obvious: a firework that sprayed sparks to amuse an emperor could also set thatched roofs ablaze within a fortress.

Chinese gunpowder weapons developed rapidly, and at the siege of Ch'i-Chou in 1221, Chinese attackers fired hundreds of gunpowder-charged arrows and even launched a true bomb, the "thunder crash."

BLAST THOSE EUROPEANS!

Gunpowder reached Europe in the thirteenth century, possibly as firecrackers brought by Flemish traveler

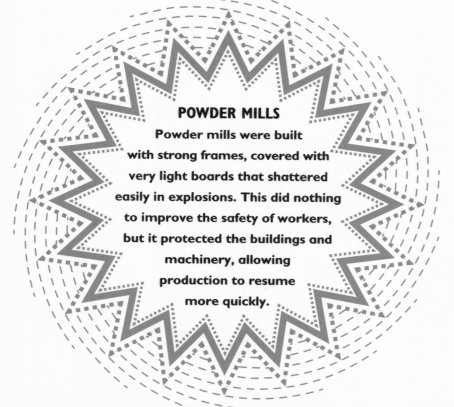

POWDER MILLS
Powder mills were built with strong frames, covered with very light boards that shattered easily in explosions. This did nothing to improve the safety of workers, but it protected the buildings and machinery, allowing production to resume more quickly.

William of Rubruck. Europeans immediately realized the destructive power of powder. In the Hundred Years' War (1337–1453), both French and English armies used cannons to blast through the castle walls of their foes.

Gunpowder revolutionized warfare, making it deadlier and noisier. However, gunpowder was costly: saltpeter, which made up three quarters of the powder, was fiendishly hard to obtain. The process of extracting it from soil soaked in dung and urine was slow and laborious and produced only tiny amounts of the precious crystals.

Victory in war came to depend on access to saltpeter. In August 1775, George Washington's revolutionary army had just 32 barrels of gunpowder, while the English, world leaders in making saltpeter, had ample supplies. If Holland and France had not smuggled 1,000 tons of saltpeter and powder to the rebels, Americans might now be saluting a British flag.

ENTERTAINING DETONATIONS

Advances in chemistry in the mid-nineteenth century led to new, stronger explosives, but they did not entirely eliminate gunpowder. The ancient Chinese "fire potion" still powers fireworks, and warfare reenactors continue using it to charge and fire their vintage weapons.

DUNG
To make the ton of powder with which Guy Fawkes planned to blow up England's king and Parliament in 1605, about 150 tons of foul-smelling dung and soil needed to be collected and processed.

FIREWORKS

The pyrotechnic rocket, the most common type of firework, is made from a paper tube packed with gunpowder, which propels the rocket into the air.

NOSE CONE
Ensures the firework flies smoothly in the right direction

CARDBOARD TUBE
Holds the firework together

STAR EFFECTS
Provide the color and noise

ROCKET MOTOR TUBE
Holds the explosives in place

DELAY
Slow-burning gunpowder that controls the timing of the explosion(s)

BLACK POWDER
Faster-burning gunpowder: the propellant that lifts the firework 300 feet (100 meters) into the air

CHOKE
Boosts the lift by funneling the rocket exhaust through a small hole

FUSE
The part of the firework that is lit

FUSE COVER
Removed before the firework is lit

THE CHEMISTRY OF COLORED FIREWORKS

RED	**ORANGE**	**YELLOW**
STRONTIUM	STRONTIUM & SODIUM	SODIUM
LIME	**GREEN**	**BLUE**
BARIUM & CALCIUM	BARIUM	COPPER
PURPLE	**GOLD**	**SILVER**
STRONTIUM & COPPER	CARBON	TITANIUM

Each effect is made up of a ball containing a metal colorant.

TYPES OF FIREWORK EFFECTS

FISH

PALM

WILLOW

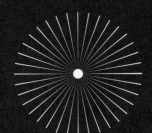
CHRYSANTHEMUM

PEONY

PISTIL

STROBE

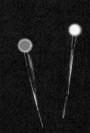
COMET

CROSETTE

BROCADE

FIREWORKS MAY BE PRETTY, BUT THE EXPLOSIVES THEY CONTAIN CAN CAUSE SEVERE BURNS. LEAVE IT TO ADULTS TO HANDLE THEM, AND NEVER PLAY WITH THEM OR TAKE THEM APART.

THE COMPASS

A needle that always points in the same direction first enchanted the people of China some 2,200 years ago. But the compass remained merely a magical novelty until sailors showed how it could revolutionize ocean travel.

LODESTONE MAY BE just a common gray rock, but it has a remarkable property: it attracts iron objects. Hung on a thread, a small piece of this magnetite aligns itself with the earth's natural magnetism, pointing north–south.

This strange ability intrigued Chinese fortune-tellers of the Han Dynasty, and by the first century CE they were demonstrating it with a spinning spoon that settled with its handle to the south. Within 1,000 years, Chinese travelers were using these predecessors of the compass to find their route when clouds obscured the sun or stars. It was in Europe, however, that the compass's potential for direction-finding was first really exploited. It is not clear whether Europeans learned of the compass from the Chinese or whether the device was independently invented on opposite sides of the world. But at the end of the twelfth century, English scholar Alexander Neckam referred to a north-pointing needle that sailors used "when the world is wrapped up in the darkness of the shades of night."

COMPASS DISASTER
Compasses are useless unless they work. After a British fleet ran aground on the rocky Isles of Scilly in 1707, drowning almost 2,000 sailors, the navy tested 145 of the ships' compasses. Only three worked properly.

WINTER SAILING

The compass was to have far-reaching consequences for world exploration, but its impact was felt first in the Mediterranean. Mariners there had been confidently crossing the inland sea since the dawn of sailing ships, using the sun and stars as their guide. But traditionally they hauled their ships from the water in winter, when cloudy skies made navigation more difficult. The compass swiftly changed this. During the course of the thirteenth century, mariners of Venice, Pisa, and Genoa began sailing in the

> **"The compass is the means to show mariners how to go in bad weather as in good."**
> **FROM JOHN FORSYTH MEIGS'S**
> ***THE STORY OF THE SEAMEN,** 1924*

winter months. The ability to sail safely for longer doubled the quantity of cargo that merchants could transport, establishing these cities as the first seafaring superpowers.

By the time Christopher Columbus set sail from Spain in 1492, navigating by compass was a mature technology. Though the explorer bragged that he could navigate by the stars and sun, it was the compass that really guided Columbus to the "new world," and added a whole new continent to maps of our planet.

A BETTER COMPASS

The compass remained the mariner's most important instrument until the dawn of the twentieth century, despite two major drawbacks: it rarely points exactly to the north, and the needle's direction is affected by iron objects in the ship's hull. The non-magnetic gyrocompass, which uses a spinning disc to find true north, solved both problems in 1906.

Today, travelers by land, sea, and air rely on satellite navigation to find their way. Yet all ships, however large, still carry a magnetic compass—just in case.

SUNSTONE
Viking navigators of the eleventh century may have used a different rock for navigation. Transparent calcite crystals turn brighter when angled to face the sun, even if it is hidden by clouds.

THE EARTH'S MAGNETIC FIELD

The earth spins around an axis that passes through the geographic North and South Poles. The magnetic poles, to which compasses point, are separated from the geographic poles by about 11° — and they move constantly.

MAGNETIC FIELD

Magnetic North Pole

Geographic North Pole

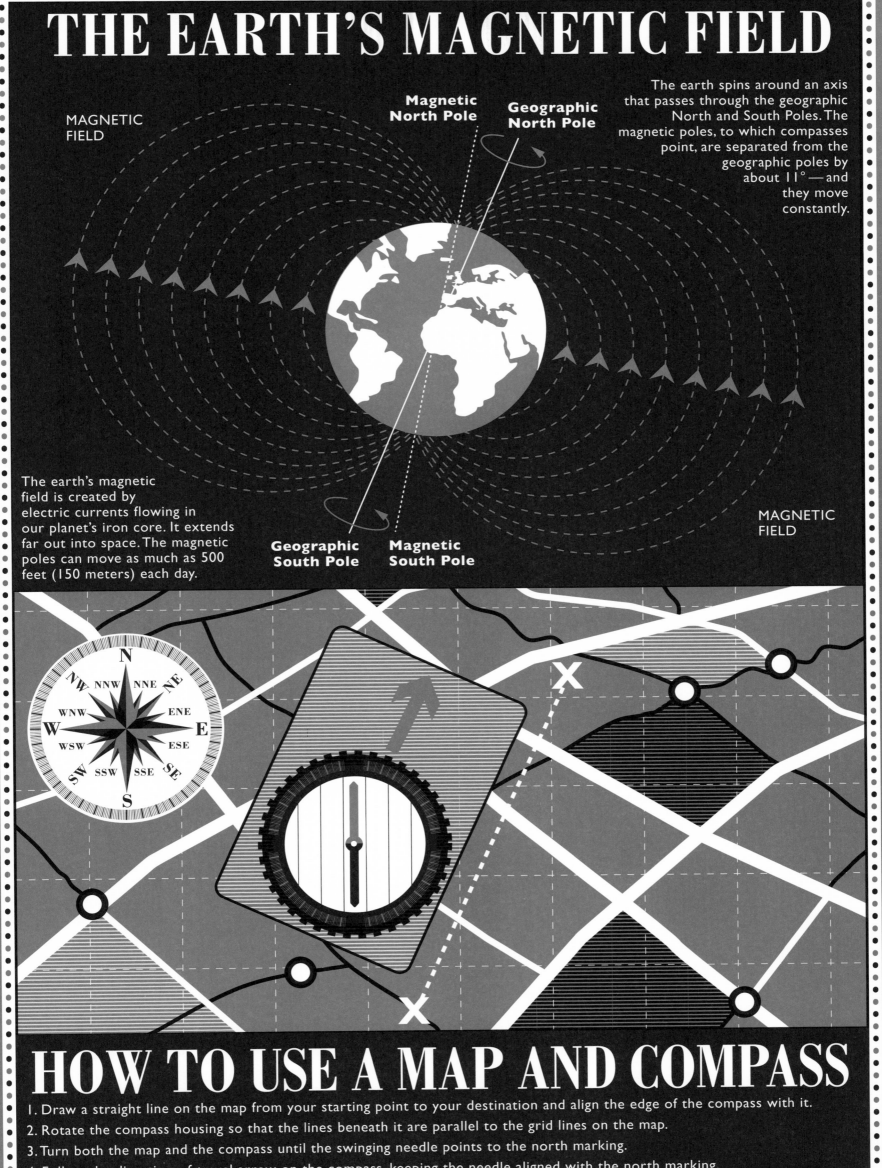

The earth's magnetic field is created by electric currents flowing in our planet's iron core. It extends far out into space. The magnetic poles can move as much as 500 feet (150 meters) each day.

Geographic South Pole

Magnetic South Pole

MAGNETIC FIELD

HOW TO USE A MAP AND COMPASS

1. Draw a straight line on the map from your starting point to your destination and align the edge of the compass with it.

2. Rotate the compass housing so that the lines beneath it are parallel to the grid lines on the map.

3. Turn both the map and the compass until the swinging needle points to the north marking.

4. Follow the direction-of-travel arrow on the compass, keeping the needle aligned with the north marking.

PRINTING

To pay off debts in 1440, a German goldsmith shared a secret with his creditors. It would completely transform religion, science, and culture.

JOHANNES GUTENBERG'S "secret" was that he had found a new way of multiplying books, which were at that time costly treasures copied out word by word using pen and ink. Much of Gutenberg's method, which we'd call printing, was not really new at all. His printing press was based on a wine press. Paper had been produced in Strasbourg, where he lived, for twenty-five years, and was beginning to replace parchment (animal skin) for writing. The sticky ink he used was borrowed from artists' oil paints. And his method of casting tiny metal letters would have been familiar to a goldsmith 500 years earlier.

CHEATED!
Alas, Gutenberg's invention did not make him rich. His scheming partner Johann Fust demanded repayment of a loan. Gutenberg lost his press, his job, and his workshop.

THE BIG IDEA

But Gutenberg's genius—and his real secret—was how he brought these skills and materials together. Metal letters rattled from his ingenious hand molds. Arranged into words, then lines, then whole pages, the type was dabbed with ink and spread with damp paper. Squeezed firmly in the press, the paper captured a perfect impression, sheet after identical sheet.

It was cleverly done, and Gutenberg turned out books at unprecedented speed from a new workshop in Mainz. He did his best to hide his invention from prying eyes, but it was futile. In 1462, Mainz was plundered in a small war, and Gutenberg's methods were soon known to the world. By 1500, there were at least 1,000 printers operating in Europe.

MORE BOOKS! MORE BOOKS!

Printing with movable type really did multiply book numbers, as Gutenberg had hoped. In the fourteenth century, fewer than 3 million books were copied by hand. In the century after his invention, some 90 million

"Gutenberg's invention . . . enables all that has been thought and said, to be preserved and transmitted to posterity."

GUILLAUME FICHET, WHO SET UP FRANCE'S FIRST PRINTING PRESS IN 1470

were printed. Printing created more than just books. Pamphlets spread shocking new ideas about science, religion, and politics, and printed newspapers began in Strasbourg in 1605.

These days, Gutenberg's printing method, now called letterpress, is used mainly by fine-art and craft printers, with most commercial printing instead using one of the six technologies shown opposite. But there was no greater change in the way we read until the introduction of computer screens in the late 1970s. Not that printing immediately swept away hand-copied books. Even after the invention of paper, many readers preferred parchment books—just as many people today prefer the printed page to the screen.

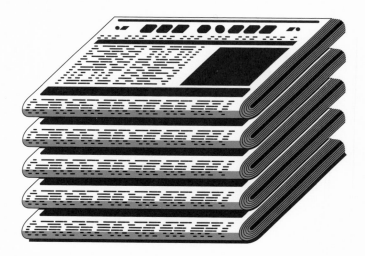

PRINTING SHAKES UP RELIGION
Before printing books, Gutenberg printed indulgences: slips of paper promising a fast track to heaven, which Christian officials sold to raise money for the Church. Soon millions of printed indulgences flooded Europe, infuriating German priest Martin Luther. In 1517, Luther rebelled, calling the Church corrupt and causing a split (called the Reformation) that divided Christians into Catholics and Protestants.

MODERN PRINTING PROCESSES

OFFSET LITHOGRAPHY

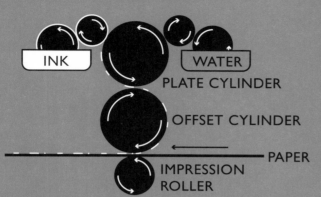

Invented at the end of the nineteenth century, lithography accounts for about half of all printing today. Areas to be printed make a greasy pattern on the printing plate. In the press, ink sticks only to the greasy parts of the dampened plate. The pattern is transferred to an offset cylinder and then onto the paper.

GRAVURE

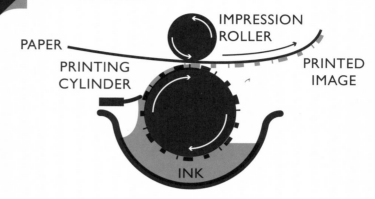

Introduced around 1900, gravure printing uses a printing plate engraved with the text and pictures. Ink sticks to these lower areas, and a blade wipes away excess ink before the paper touches the plate. Gravure gives high-quality impressions, and plates wear slowly, so the process is used to print popular magazines.

FLEXOGRAPHY

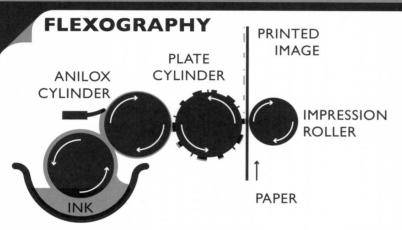

An 1890 invention, flexography prints from a raised image, like letterpress — but the printing plates are made of flexible rubber. In the press, an anilox cylinder ensures a perfectly even spread of ink. Flexography ink sticks even to shiny surfaces, such as metal and plastic, and is widely used to print on packaging.

SCREEN PRINTING

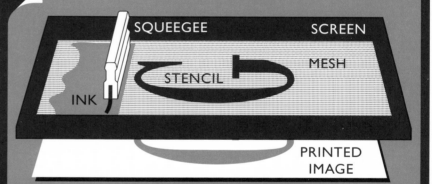

Chinese printers began using woven screens to print images more than 1,000 years ago. Areas where no ink is required are blocked off with a stencil, and a squeegee — a rubber blade — forces ink through the screen onto the paper. Because of its simplicity, screen printing is widely used by artists.

INKJET PRINTING

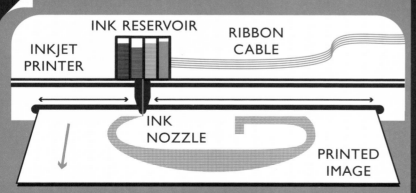

Invented about 50 years ago, inkjet printing transfers images without a printing plate by spraying onto the paper tiny ink drops colored yellow, purple, blue-green, or black. A computer controls the flow of ink, switching it on and off as the paper scrolls past the spray nozzle.

LASER PRINTING

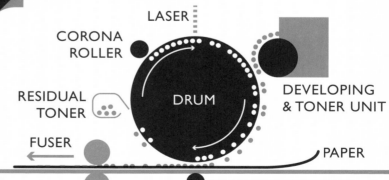

Inside a laser printer, data representing the image switches a laser beam on and off. The laser scans a drum charged with static electricity. The beam shines only on areas that must print, reversing their charge so that they attract toner particles. Heat fuses toner to paper.

LENSES

Named for the lentil that it resembles, a glass lens has an almost magical ability to capture the three-dimensional world in which we live and to transform it into a perfect flat picture.

EARLY LENSES, made of natural rock crystal, were used some 2,500 years ago to bend the sun's rays and gather them into a searing, fire-lighting pinpoint. But it was the ability of the lens to aid vision that caught the eye of observant Romans. In first-century Italy, philosophers Pliny and Seneca noticed that a water-filled glass ball enlarged what was behind it. And Emperor Nero squinted through a rounded gemstone to correct his short sight.

PERSIAN PIONEER

The scientific study of lenses began in the tenth century, when Persian mathematician Ibn Sahl wrote about their light-bending power in his paper "Burning Mirrors and Lenses." But lenses were used mostly for fire-starting, and as magnifying glasses, until craftsmen in Venice and Florence learned how to grind glass into gentle curves. These "little discs for the eyes" were the first spectacles and were common by the start of the fourteenth century.

It's a short step from correcting vision with a lens to projecting a picture: fixed in a window shutter, a lens sends an upside-down view of the

> ## "All painting is dead in comparison."
>
> **DUTCH POET CONSTANTIJN HUYGENS WHEN HE FIRST SAW A CAMERA OBSCURA IN 1622**

A UNIQUE SPECTACLE
A fourteenth-century ophthalmologist's shop in Venice was a grab bag. There was no way of testing eyes, and glass-workers had not mastered grinding lenses to a precise curve. Customers just tried on spectacles until they found a pair that worked for them.

> **OLDEST LENS**
> What was the world's first lens? The oldest surviving example is a 3,000-year-old polished circle of natural crystal discovered in 1850 in Nimrud (now in Iraq). Scientists argue over whether it was a burning glass, a magnifying glass or a monocle.

scene outside into a darkened room—known in Latin as a *camera obscura*. Italian artists realized the value of the camera obscura during the Renaissance—an explosion of knowledge that marked the beginning of the modern world. Perhaps as early as 1420 some of them used it to trace views onto their pictures, leading to a revolutionary new realism in art.

LOOKING FARTHER . . . AND CLOSER

Over the next three centuries, reason and understanding grew more important than unquestioning belief, and scientific endeavor flourished—and lenses brought another revolution. Telescopes, probably invented in the Netherlands in 1608 by spectacle-maker Hans Lippershey, allowed scientists to look outward and begin to understand the vastness of the universe. Microscopes, which appeared around the same time and place, showed scientists the tiniest details of nature.

In 1838, lenses produced one more astonishing surprise. French showman Louis Daguerre put a shiny silvered plate—which he had made sensitive to light—into a box-sized camera obscura. With it he made the image projected by the lens permanent. His "mirror with a memory," or daguerreotype—or photograph—changed forever how we look at, understand, and remember our world.

CAMERA *OBSCURA*

CAMERA OBSCURA

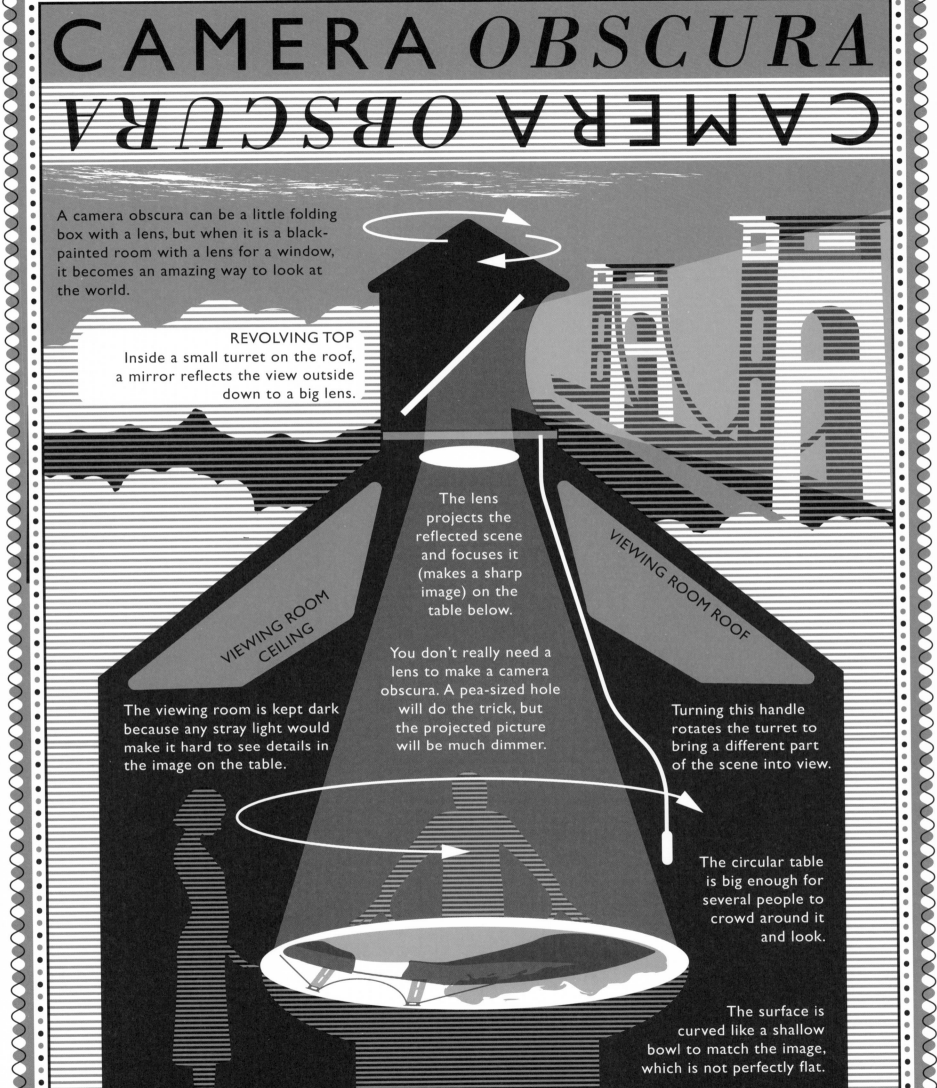

A camera obscura can be a little folding box with a lens, but when it is a black-painted room with a lens for a window, it becomes an amazing way to look at the world.

REVOLVING TOP
Inside a small turret on the roof, a mirror reflects the view outside down to a big lens.

VIEWING ROOM CEILING

VIEWING ROOM ROOF

The lens projects the reflected scene and focuses it (makes a sharp image) on the table below.

You don't really need a lens to make a camera obscura. A pea-sized hole will do the trick, but the projected picture will be much dimmer.

The viewing room is kept dark because any stray light would make it hard to see details in the image on the table.

Turning this handle rotates the turret to bring a different part of the scene into view.

The circular table is big enough for several people to crowd around it and look.

The surface is curved like a shallow bowl to match the image, which is not perfectly flat.

THE FLUSH TOILET

Human waste is something we prefer not to see, hear, touch, or smell. Flush toilets make this possible, but only when connected to an expensive and elaborate sewer system.

FLUSH TOILETS are magic-trick inventions. They take a smelly problem and—abracadabra!—make it disappear with a splash. This vanishing act has transformed the world's cities from stinking, unhealthy open sewers to the (usually) sweet-smelling places they are today. But the change was not an easy one, for the invention of the flushing toilet broke a human-waste disposal process that had worked for centuries.

FIT FOR A QUEEN

Earlier toilets didn't wash away human waste. Instead they deposited it into cesspits—closed tanks in gardens and cellars. Emptying these pits was the nasty job of "night-soil men," who dug out the waste, loaded it into carts, and took it to farms, where they sold it as fertilizer.

The "water closet" that ended this neat feat of recycling was the creation of Sir John Harington, a godson of England's Queen Elizabeth I. Harington built a toilet fit for a queen at the end of the sixteenth century at the royal palace in Richmond, near London. He admitted that the more often the pan was flushed, "the sweeter [it will be]," but added that one flush for every twenty uses was usually enough.

Harington's invention briefly made him famous, but it was useless outside

CHEAP AND SAFE

Supplying safe and hygienic toilets for the people who still lack them today would cost around $330 billion—less than one-sixth of the money spent worldwide every year on waging war.

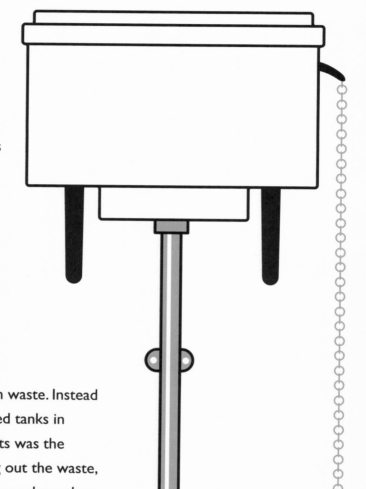
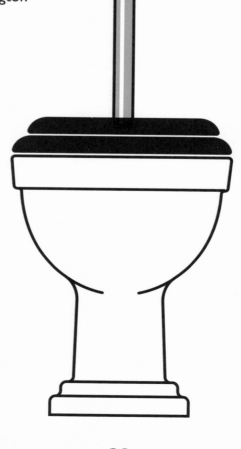

a palace, for only the wealthiest households had running water. Three centuries would pass before the flush toilet became a practical reality for most of the population. And when it did, it caused a public health disaster.

NOT THE INVENTOR

The last name of Victorian engineer Thomas Crapper has become a slang word for the toilet, but he did not invent it. He did, however, run a successful London plumbing business in the 1870s and 1880s, and supplied equipment to England's palaces.

UNINTENDED CONSEQUENCES

When Londoners began flushing their toilets with water, the cesspits overflowed. To solve this problem, plumbers diverted sewage into street drains that had been built to carry only rainwater. As a result, London's wells and river became stinking, unhealthy drains. Hot summers brought a crisis: polluted by sewage, London's drinking water poisoned its citizens. In 1853, 10,000 people died when cholera struck the city. Lawmakers tackled the problem by building a citywide sewer system. It was enormously expensive, but it worked. Large cities in America and Europe faced similar sanitation problems, and one by one they adopted the same solution. The combination of flush toilets and sewers made cities healthy places to live.

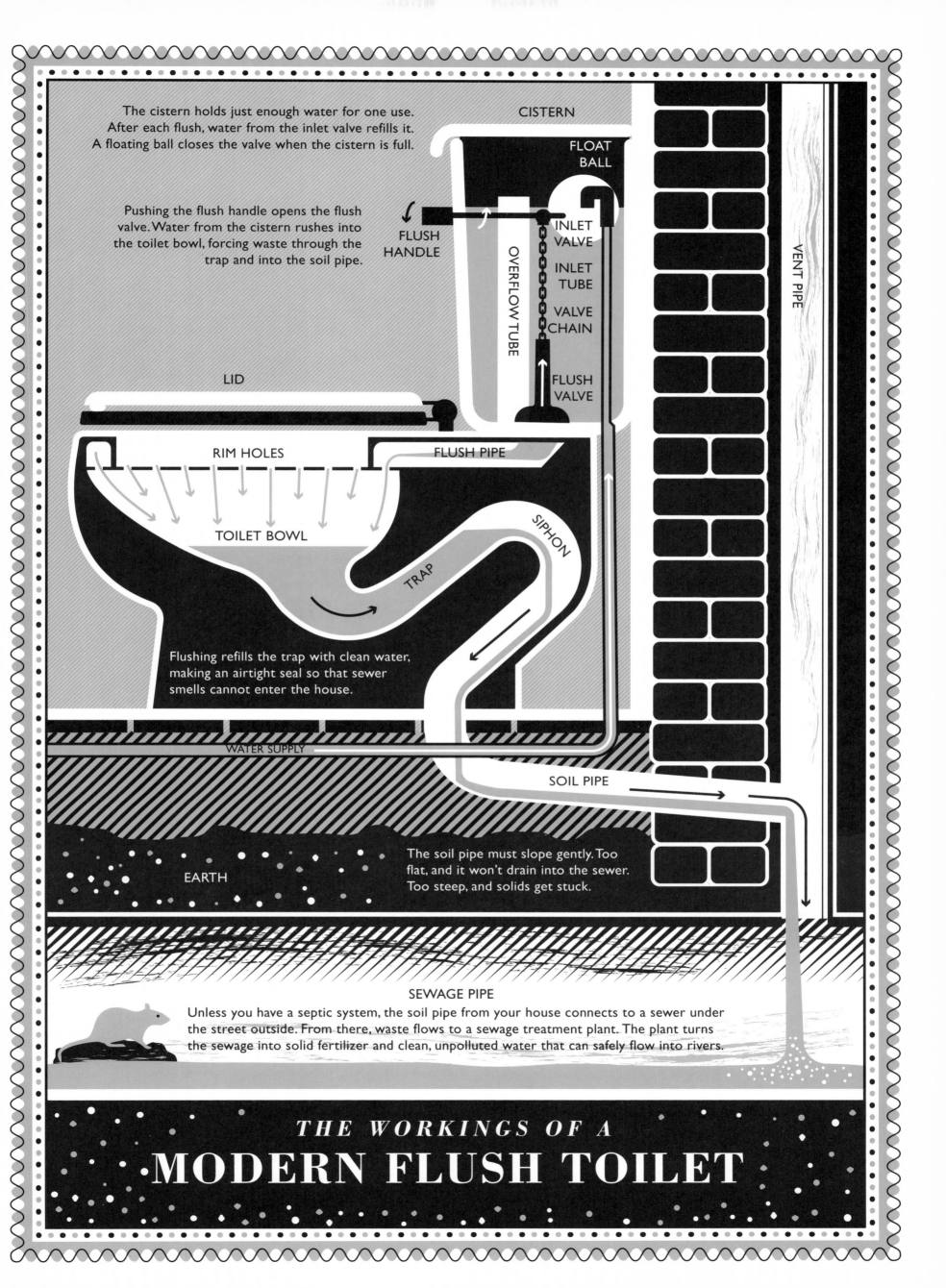

The cistern holds just enough water for one use. After each flush, water from the inlet valve refills it. A floating ball closes the valve when the cistern is full.

Pushing the flush handle opens the flush valve. Water from the cistern rushes into the toilet bowl, forcing waste through the trap and into the soil pipe.

CISTERN

FLOAT BALL

FLUSH HANDLE

INLET VALVE

INLET TUBE

VALVE CHAIN

FLUSH VALVE

OVERFLOW TUBE

VENT PIPE

LID

RIM HOLES

FLUSH PIPE

TOILET BOWL

SIPHON

TRAP

Flushing refills the trap with clean water, making an airtight seal so that sewer smells cannot enter the house.

WATER SUPPLY

SOIL PIPE

EARTH

The soil pipe must slope gently. Too flat, and it won't drain into the sewer. Too steep, and solids get stuck.

SEWAGE PIPE

Unless you have a septic system, the soil pipe from your house connects to a sewer under the street outside. From there, waste flows to a sewage treatment plant. The plant turns the sewage into solid fertilizer and clean, unpolluted water that can safely flow into rivers.

THE WORKINGS OF A
MODERN FLUSH TOILET

INOCULATION

A milkmaid's boast may have inspired an eighteenth-century doctor to prevent deadly smallpox by infecting patients with milder cowpox. This inoculation, and the innovations that followed it, saved countless lives.

WORKING FROM AN OFFICE in a small town in the U.K. in the late 1700s, Edward Jenner was just an ordinary family doctor. However, he had an inquiring mind and had been privileged to study medicine with some of the most eminent physicians of his time. When he became interested in the popular notion that milkmaids did not suffer from smallpox, he investigated the claim in a systematic and scientific way (see opposite).

Jenner reported his discoveries on inoculation to the Royal Society, Britain's foremost scientific institution, but was advised that he did not have enough proof that the method worked. When he had repeated the experiment successfully several more times, Jenner had a paper describing his work printed and published at his own expense.

IS IT SAFE?

Jenner's experiment was too risky to be permitted today, but he had good reason to be confident that it would not harm his patients. Long before Jenner, traditional healers had used similar methods. Back in 1000 CE, Chinese doctors puffed ground smallpox scabs up patients' noses to protect against the disease. Around 1717, English traveler Lady Mary Wortley Montagu watched inoculation in Turkey and had her own children protected.

LIFESAVING JABS

So Jenner wasn't the first to prevent smallpox, but he persuaded doubting doctors that vaccination—from *vacca*, the Latin word for cow—worked, and his method

> ## "Vaccination gives no protection whatever."
>
> **ALFRED RUSSEL WALLACE, AN OUTSPOKEN AND MISTAKEN OPPONENT OF VACCINATION, IN 1898**

eventually became the most popular way to protect against smallpox. Jenner's experiment started a battle that ended only in 1980 with the worldwide eradication of smallpox, which nobody anywhere need ever die of again.

Researchers who followed Jenner improved inoculation, making the method work for different illnesses by injecting patients with a dead or weakened form of the disease. An estimated 2 to 3 million lives are saved around the world each year by inoculation against twenty-six diseases, including measles, whooping cough, and tetanus. This is a huge achievement, but researchers believe that inoculation can do even more. The World Health Organization is battling to eliminate other diseases. Thirty years ago there were estimated to be 350,000 cases of polio each year. Today there are fewer than two dozen cases worldwide, and soon the disease could—like smallpox—be just a memory.

HIDE OF A HERO

Milkmaid Sarah Nelmes caught the cowpox from Blossom the cow. Blossom's hide still decorates the library wall at St George's Hospital in London, the medical school where Jenner studied.

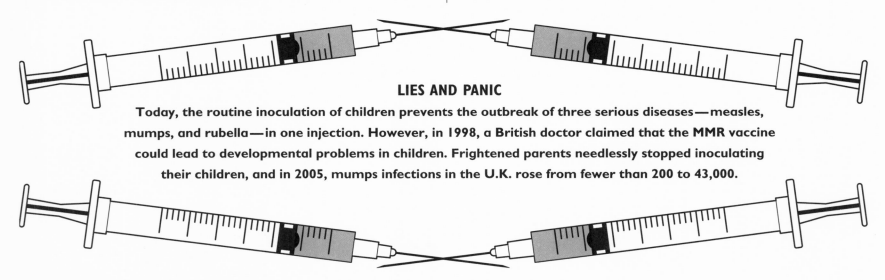

LIES AND PANIC

Today, the routine inoculation of children prevents the outbreak of three serious diseases—measles, mumps, and rubella—in one injection. However, in 1998, a British doctor claimed that the MMR vaccine could lead to developmental problems in children. Frightened parents needlessly stopped inoculating their children, and in 2005, mumps infections in the U.K. rose from fewer than 200 to 43,000.

Edward Jenner
AND THE STORY OF VACCINATION

As a teenage surgeon's apprentice in 1766, Edward Jenner overheard a milkmaid say, "I cannot [suffer from smallpox], for I have had cowpox. I shall never have an ugly pockmarked face."

Thirty years later, Dr Jenner decided to test this idea.

Another milkmaid, Sarah Nelmes, had caught cowpox from a cow she milked.

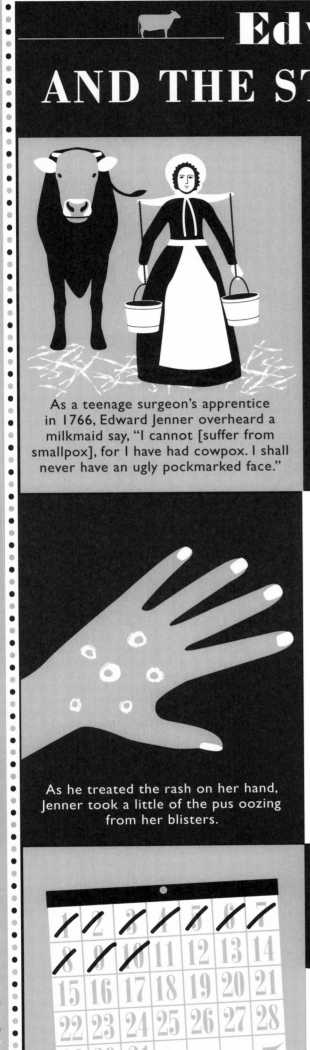

As he treated the rash on her hand, Jenner took a little of the pus oozing from her blisters.

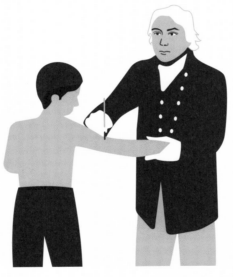

He rubbed it into scratches he made on the arm of his gardener's son, eight-year-old James Phipps.

As Jenner expected, the boy got a fever, and his armpits hurt.

In 10 days, James had recovered from these symptoms of cowpox, and six weeks later, Jenner tried a risky experiment. . . .

He scratched James with pus from a patient infected with smallpox. This disease kills a third of those who catch it and often leaves survivors blind and covered in scars.

Fortunately, Jenner was proved right. The boy was immune — protected — from the more serious disease because he had suffered the lesser one.

AGRICULTURAL MACHINERY

The first harvesting machines were large, expensive, and unreliable, but for the farmers who could afford them they replaced something even more expensive and unreliable—the exhausted farm laborer.

PULLED BY AN OX or a donkey some 4,000 years ago, the plow was the very first farming machine. By cutting and turning the soil, the plow buried weeds and brought fertile earth to the surface. Following the plow with a harrow—a rack of downward-pointing spikes—prepared a field for sowing with seeds. However, it was not until much later that inventors turned their attention to the harvesting of the crop.

HARD HARVESTING

Winnowing, or removing the chaff from the grain, was the first harvesting process to be mechanized. Since around the third century, Chinese farmers had been cleaning their rice crops with mechanical fans. European farmers learned of this technology from Jesuit missionaries who returned from the East with the machines in the early eighteenth century, and they adapted them for wheat as "fantackle and chogger" winnowers. Scottish mechanic Michael Menzies built a machine for threshing in the 1730s, and reaping machines, pulled by horses, were invented a century later. A reaper made in around 1826 by another Scotsman, Patrick Bell, was widely copied because he failed to patent it.

All of these machines reduced the exhausting labor of the harvest. Bell's reaping machine could cut as much wheat in an hour as a man with a scythe could cut in a day, reducing

the work by two-thirds. Mechanization took away the jobs of many thousands of farm laborers, however, and in 1830, groups of them in southern and eastern England rioted, smashing machines in the process.

KILLING WIDOWS
In Japan threshing machines were nicknamed *goke taoshi*, or "widow-killers," because threshing was traditionally the work of old women, who were not strong enough to operate the new devices and could find no other employment.

MACHINES MARCH ON

Despite this opposition, further mechanization was unstoppable. Just 10 years after Bell's reaper, machines that combined cutting, threshing, and winnowing appeared. These "combine harvesters" were at first pulled by teams of mules or horses, then by steam engines, and later by gas-powered tractors. Combines were first used in the United States and Australia, where huge flat fields lent themselves to mechanization, but they soon spread around the world. Modern combines resemble the early machines, but technology has made them more productive and automatic. Operators ride in air-conditioned comfort, and their machines use satellite navigation to map and weigh the crop so that the following year's fertilizer is spread only where it is needed. Further automation will soon produce the "farmerless field"—driverless machines have already plowed, planted, and harvested a crop in Shropshire, England.

SUPERSTITIOUS HARVEST
Inventors of harvest machines had to be secretive, because some farmers shared a superstitious belief that mechanization worked against nature. Bell made his first trials in a barn, then carried out field tests after dark.

> "Horses became giddy from walking in endless circles to drive the first threshing machines."
>
> **FROM G. E. FUSSELL'S *THE FARMER'S TOOLS*, 1952**

THE COMBINE
HARVESTER

The combine harvester uses an ingenious series of machines to reproduce the three harvesting tasks that were previously carried out by hand. The head at the front cuts a swathe through the field up to 40 feet (12 meters) wide. After processing, the harvester stores grain in a tank and sprays chopped straw waste onto the field.

REAPING

To harvest wheat by hand, a farm laborer bends to cut the stalks off close to ground level using a reaping hook, then stacks them to dry.

THRESHING

Beating the dry crop with a jointed pole removes straw and loosens chaff—the scaly inedible coating that covers the edible seeds.

WINNOWING

WIND   WHEAT   CHAFF

To separate the chaff from the grain, workers traditionally tossed it in the air in a breeze. The wind blows the lighter chaff aside.

GRAIN LIFT
A conveyor carries grain up to a storage tank.

GRAIN TANK
When the tank is full, a tractor brings a trailer alongside and the grain is unloaded.

STRAW WALKER
Stalks move back along another conveyor.

DRIVER'S CABIN

GRAIN TANK

GRAIN LIFT

THRESHER
A drum-like thresher separates the grain from the stalks.

THRESHER

STRAW WALKER

STRAW CHOPPER

SIEVES

REEL

FEEDER

FAN

CUTTER

REEL
Turning slowly, the reel pushes the crop into the cutter.

CUTTER
The scissor-like blades of the cutter snip off the stalks near the ground.

FEEDER
A conveyor lifts the crop into the processing section of the harvester.

FAN
Blowing air through the grain winnows out more chaff.

SIEVES
Sifting the grain separates stones and some of the chaff.

STRAW CHOPPER
The straw is waste, so it is cut up and sprayed onto the field.

STEAM POWER

Three hundred years ago, the white plume from a kettle's spout kicked off a worldwide industial revolution. Today, steam power seems like a relic from a bygone age . . . but it still keeps the lights on.

FROM THE DAWN of human history all the way up until the eighteenth century, the only aids to human and animal muscle were wind and water. Captured by windmills and waterwheels, they spun labor-saving machinery to make heavy work almost effortless. But nature is fickle, and calm or drought could bring a productive mill to a halt. Steam changed all this, providing labor-saving power almost on demand.

MINE CRAFT

The steam age began not with a railway locomotive but with a water pump. Around 1712, English ironmonger and preacher Thomas Newcomen devised a way of moving a piston by first filling the cylinder it sealed with steam, then spraying in water to create a vacuum. The piston rocked a beam, which pulled a rod, which ran down a mine shaft to a water pump—which drained the mine. It was an inefficient and fuel-hungry beast, but for more than half a century Newcomen's "Invention for Raising Water by Fire" remained the sole means of "unwatering" deep mines. This method was improved only after Scottish engineer James Watt received a scale model to repair in 1763. He quickly recognized that it was hugely wasteful of energy, as the engine's cylinder had to be heated then cooled

SNEAKY OPERATOR
To keep Newcomen's early pumps running, small boys were tasked with constantly opening and closing valves. The story goes that in 1713, one such boy, Humphrey Potter, wanted to leave the pump to play with his friends, so he tied strings from the overhead beam to the operating valves. This made the pump work automatically.

STEAMY INSPIRATION
In a legend explaining the origin of Newcomen's mine pump, the inventor watched steam in his teakettle lift the lid.

on each stroke. By condensing the steam in a separate chamber, Watt greatly improved the pump's efficiency.

HORSE POWER AND WATTS
The first steam engine did the work of five horses. By 1800, the best steam engine was stronger than 170 horses. "Horsepower" became a measure of an engine's strength that is still in use today. And Watt's name became a power unit too: 735 watts = 1 horsepower.

PUFFING TO GLORY

Watt's engines powered the industrial revolution—a century of radical change that replaced manual labor with machines and revolutionized transportation. From 1781, steam engines spun machinery in mills, and they were soon made small enough to drive moving vehicles. The changes had an impact far beyond Britain: over the next half-century Watt sold 110 machines to nineteen foreign countries. Famously, locomotives transformed travel and completely rearranged where people lived, worked, and relaxed.

Steam became the primary source of power. Of course, when electric power came on the scene in the 1880s, all this changed. Or did it? The principal way of generating electricity was by boiling water to make . . . steam. A jet of steam spun a turbine connected to a generator. Even today, steam turbines in coal, gas, and nuclear plants generate four-fifths of the world's power.

Newcomen's atmospheric
STEAM ENGINE

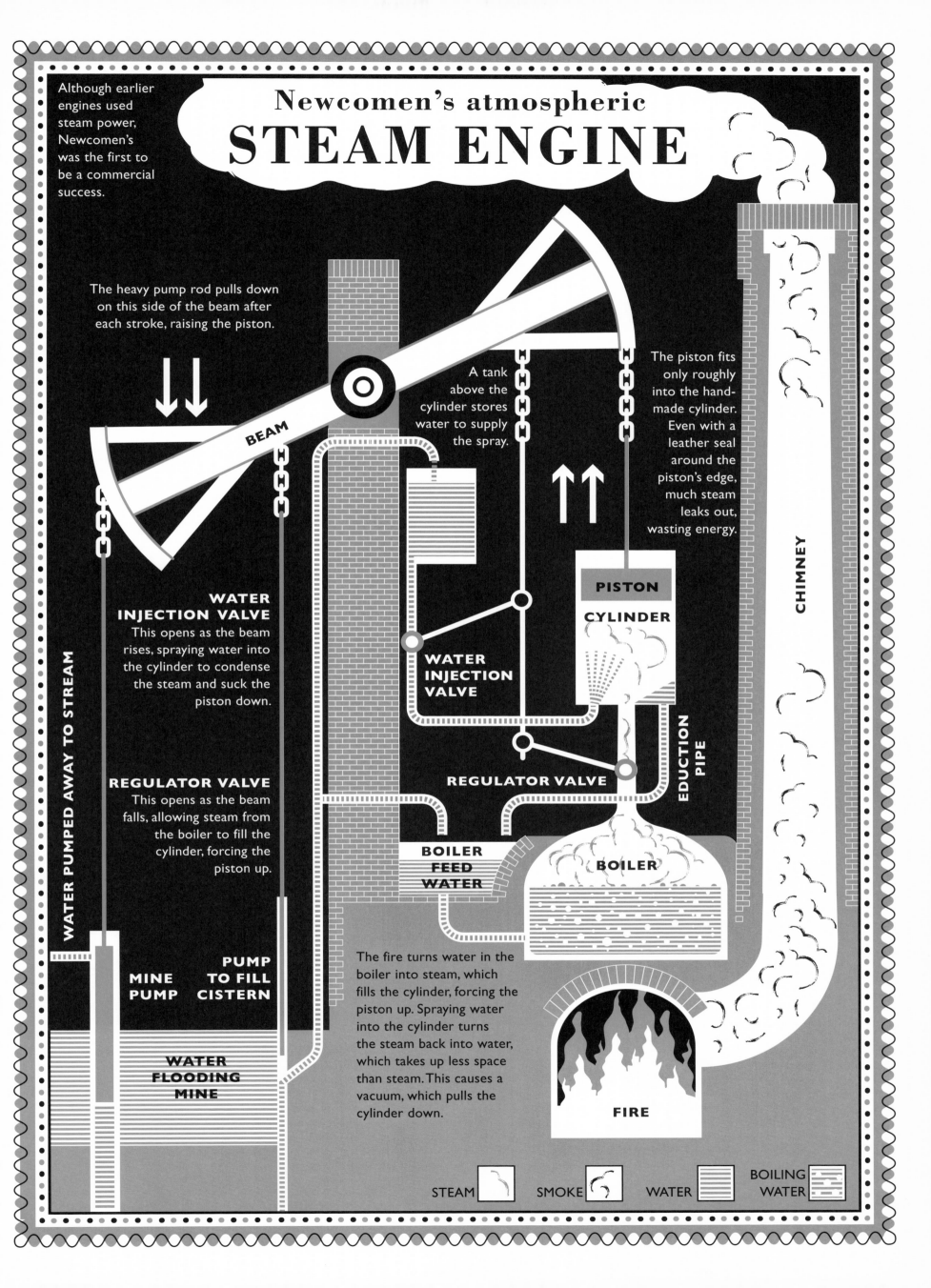

The heavy pump rod pulls down on this side of the beam after each stroke, raising the piston.

BEAM

A tank above the cylinder stores water to supply the spray.

The piston fits only roughly into the hand-made cylinder. Even with a leather seal around the piston's edge, much steam leaks out, wasting energy.

CHIMNEY

WATER INJECTION VALVE
This opens as the beam rises, spraying water into the cylinder to condense the steam and suck the piston down.

PISTON

CYLINDER

WATER INJECTION VALVE

REGULATOR VALVE
This opens as the beam falls, allowing steam from the boiler to fill the cylinder, forcing the piston up.

REGULATOR VALVE

EDUCTION PIPE

WATER PUMPED AWAY TO STREAM

BOILER FEED WATER

BOILER

MINE PUMP

PUMP TO FILL CISTERN

The fire turns water in the boiler into steam, which fills the cylinder, forcing the piston up. Spraying water into the cylinder turns the steam back into water, which takes up less space than steam. This causes a vacuum, which pulls the cylinder down.

WATER FLOODING MINE

FIRE

STEAM   SMOKE   WATER   BOILING WATER

THE NAIL

*The humble nail changed the course of history,
sparking revolutionary discontent and creating the wooden
frame buildings that shaped American towns and villages.*

NAILS ARE AMONG the oldest of building materials. The ancient Greeks and Romans used them, but in small quantities, for metal was costly. In fact, until the nineteenth century, nails were so expensive that European carpenters rarely hammered them into traditional wooden buildings. Instead they painstakingly sawed and chipped the ends of huge timbers into complex joints, fixing them with oak pegs. Nails were valuable not only because metal was scarce, but also because making a nail was hard work. A skilled blacksmith might make only 200 to 300 a day.

NO HOMEGROWN NAILS

By the eighteenth century, nails had become a valuable British export. This made them a central issue in the American Revolution. Britain's lawmakers insisted that settlers in America bought all manufactured goods from Britain: politician Lord Chatham declared that "the colonists had no right to manufacture even a nail for a horse-shoe."

After winning the revolution—and the right to make nails and anything else they wanted—Americans streamlined the nail-making craft, using simple mechanical aids to speed it up. Then, around 1796, Massachusetts goldsmith Jacob Perkins invented a machine that cut nails and put heads on them in two steps. Perkins's machines turned out a million nails every five days, and nail prices plunged. In 1790, a pound of nails (just under half a kilogram) cost 25 cents. By 1828, the price had dropped to 8 cents, and by 1842 it was 3 cents.

DATE THAT NAIL
Nail shapes are so distinctive that archaeologists can use them to date a building's construction, sometimes to within a year.

"I am myself a nail-maker."
U.S. PRESIDENT THOMAS JEFFERSON IN 1795

A NEW KIND OF HOUSE

Cheap nails in turn transformed construction. In 1830s Chicago, carpenters began making house frames by nailing together many small boards instead of jointing a few heavy beams. In just a week, this technique could create a house that looked so light and graceful it seemed like it might blow away on a breeze. Critics laughed at "balloon framing"—but then used it themselves, as building houses this way cut the cost by more than a third. It required little skill, too: a man and a boy could do the work of twenty skilled craftsmen.

Very soon, up to four out of every five houses in the United States used balloon frames: the machine-made nail had created a completely new architectural style. Light, flat-walled timber buildings are treasured today as a uniquely American tradition, but the nail-and-plank method has become a standard way of making houses and other small buildings all over the world.

BURST-PROOF BALLOON
Despite their appearance, the nailed-together houses were incredibly strong. As Thomas Eddy Tallmadge said in his book *Architecture in Old Chicago,* "Many a 'balloon construction' house, like a gigantic tumbleweed, has rolled along the prairie under the urging of a tornado, without serious injury to the house."

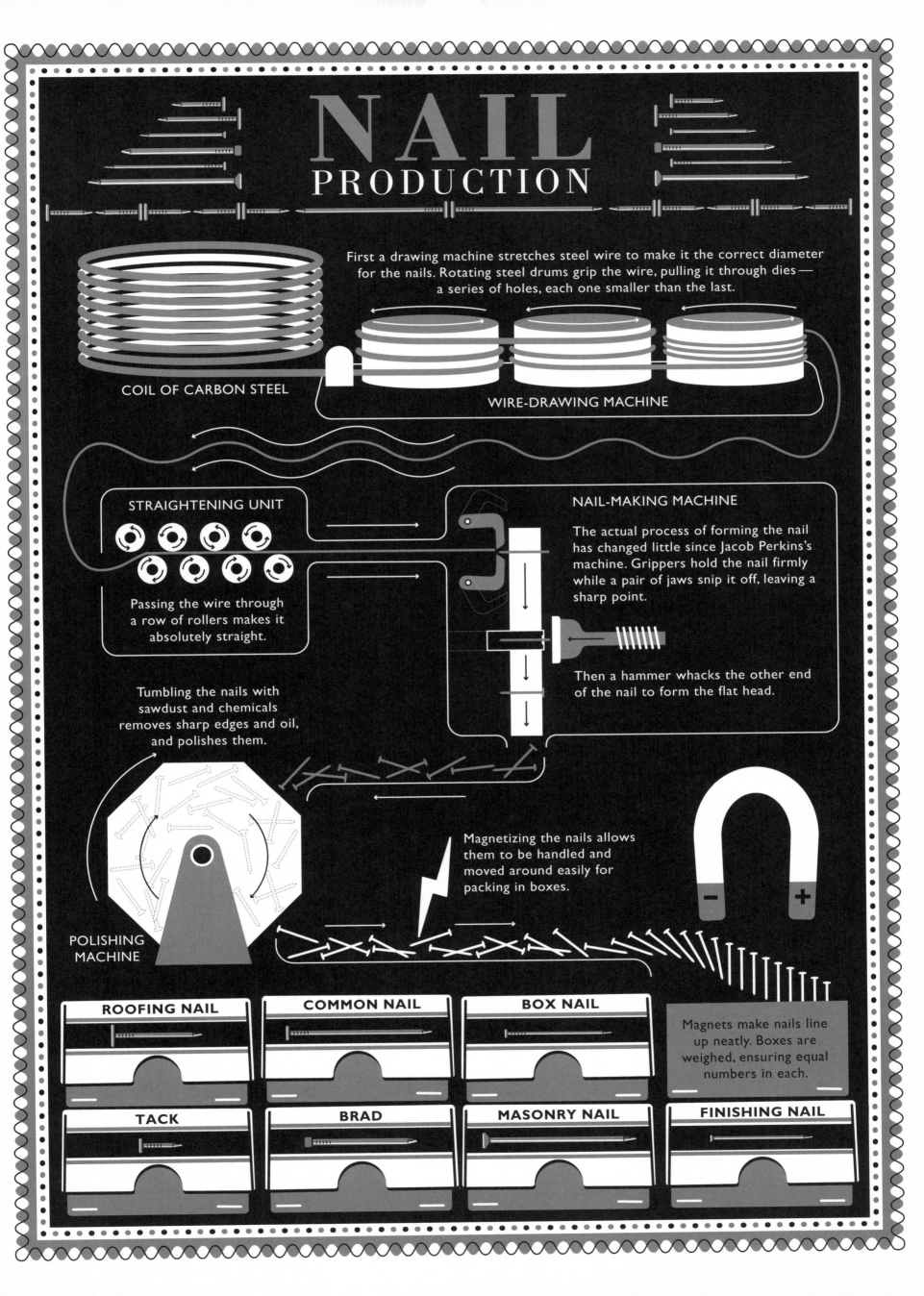

NAIL
PRODUCTION

First a drawing machine stretches steel wire to make it the correct diameter for the nails. Rotating steel drums grip the wire, pulling it through dies — a series of holes, each one smaller than the last.

COIL OF CARBON STEEL

WIRE-DRAWING MACHINE

STRAIGHTENING UNIT

Passing the wire through a row of rollers makes it absolutely straight.

NAIL-MAKING MACHINE

The actual process of forming the nail has changed little since Jacob Perkins's machine. Grippers hold the nail firmly while a pair of jaws snip it off, leaving a sharp point.

Then a hammer whacks the other end of the nail to form the flat head.

Tumbling the nails with sawdust and chemicals removes sharp edges and oil, and polishes them.

Magnetizing the nails allows them to be handled and moved around easily for packing in boxes.

POLISHING MACHINE

− +

ROOFING NAIL COMMON NAIL BOX NAIL

Magnets make nails line up neatly. Boxes are weighed, ensuring equal numbers in each.

TACK BRAD MASONRY NAIL FINISHING NAIL

HIGH-RISE BUILDINGS

Cheap, abundant steel gave engineers and architects a new ability to create slender city towers in the mid-nineteenth century. But without elevators, they would have been almost empty.

A FLIGHT OF STAIRS is not a concern for a fit person, but five flights will leave most people panting. In early-nineteenth-century America, the effort of climbing stairs meant that the most popular rooms—and the highest rents—were on the lowest floors of large hotels or office blocks. The invention of the elevator took the work out of getting to the top, but elevators had a serious image problem. Passengers feared that if the rope supporting the elevator car broke, they would plunge screaming down the elevator shaft.

A SAFER RIDE

In 1852, American elevator manufacturer Elisha Otis devised a "safety elevator," which had built-in brakes that gripped the sides of the elevator shaft. The brakes released if the rope supporting the car was tight. If the rope snapped, the brakes sprang out, stopping the car's descent.

Otis promoted it with a breathtaking stunt at a New York exhibition. As he rose high above the crowds in an open elevator, an assistant above him dramatically slashed the cable. The elevator fell just centimeters before stopping safely. Impressed, developers rushed to install elevators in new buildings. After 1860, practically every New York hotel had elevators.

BIRTH OF THE SKYSCRAPER

The story might have ended there, but the invention of the safety elevator was just the beginning of a much taller tale. The price of

land in cities was spiraling as new railways and telegraph lines made travel and communication easier. Construction methods changed, too. Older buildings were no taller than five stories because of the thick masonry walls needed to hold them up. This reduced the floor space available. But in the middle of the century, the Bessemer process, a new way of making steel, cut the price of construction girders. Developers began using steel frames, which could support a building of almost any height.

Without elevators, tall buildings were pointless, as nobody wanted rooms above the fifth floor. Elevators reversed this. Upper floors were high above the noise and filth of the street and had better light; suddenly the penthouse was where everyone wanted to live and work. Elevators literally changed the city skyline, allowing skyscrapers to thrust upward in jagged, dramatic towers of glass, steel, and concrete.

SEGREGATED ELEVATORS

In nineteenth-century America it was considered improper for a woman to be alone in a room with a man she did not know. Chicago's Pacific Hotel, built in 1870, had one elevator for gentlemen and couples and a separate one for unaccompanied ladies.

> "When they find themselves a little crowded, they simply tilt a street on end and call it a skyscraper."
>
> **SCOTTISH JOURNALIST WILLIAM ARCHER, REFERRING TO NEW YORKERS IN 1899**

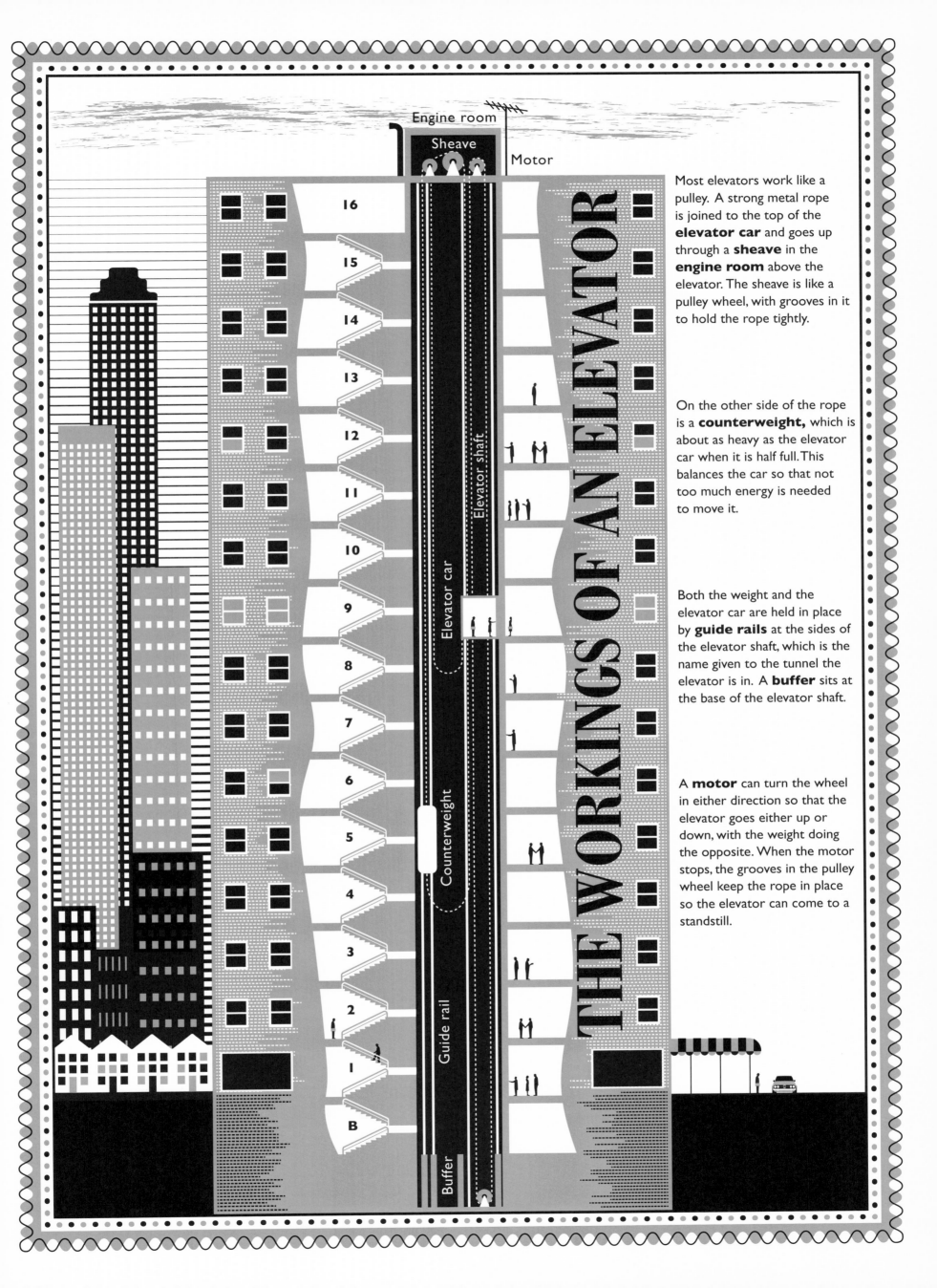

THE WORKINGS OF AN ELEVATOR

Engine room

Sheave

Motor

16
15
14
13
12
11
10
9
8
7
6
5
4
3
2
1
B

Elevator car

Elevator shaft

Counterweight

Guide rail

Buffer

Most elevators work like a pulley. A strong metal rope is joined to the top of the **elevator car** and goes up through a **sheave** in the **engine room** above the elevator. The sheave is like a pulley wheel, with grooves in it to hold the rope tightly.

On the other side of the rope is a **counterweight,** which is about as heavy as the elevator car when it is half full. This balances the car so that not too much energy is needed to move it.

Both the weight and the elevator car are held in place by **guide rails** at the sides of the elevator shaft, which is the name given to the tunnel the elevator is in. A **buffer** sits at the base of the elevator shaft.

A **motor** can turn the wheel in either direction so that the elevator goes either up or down, with the weight doing the opposite. When the motor stops, the grooves in the pulley wheel keep the rope in place so the elevator can come to a standstill.

THE TELEPHONE

The origins of many vital inventions are confused or disputed.
At least half a dozen different inventors claimed to have devised a
telephone, although we remember the name of only one of them.

IT'S TOUGH to imagine life without phones, as our cell phones do almost everything for us. In addition to keeping us constantly in touch with friends and family, they are web browsers, calendars, translators, travel guides—and can even adjust our thermostats when we're not at home.

Telephones (the original wired kind) were famously the invention of Alexander Graham Bell. In 1875, Bell had been trying to find a way of sending multiple messages down a single wire. When his assistant plucked a metal reed next to a wire coil, the electric current this produced traveled down a connected cable, creating a buzz on a similar reed in an adjacent room. It was the "Eureka!" moment that revealed the potential of the phone. Further experiments enabled Bell to perfect and patent the "apparatus for transmitting vocal or other sounds telegraphically"—and make his fortune.

> ## "Harrumph! It's only a toy."
> **ALEXANDER GRAHAM BELL'S FATHER-IN-LAW,**
> **GARDINER GREENE HUBBARD, WHEN SHOWN**
> **A TELEPHONE PROTOTYPE IN 1876**

WAS HE FIRST?

It is a neat tale, but it's only part of a more complicated story. Twenty years earlier, poor Italian immigrant Antonio Meucci installed a working telephone in his New York home. Lacking financing and speaking little English, the inventor struggled with the patent process that would have protected his invention. When Bell's phone appeared, Meucci (and others) unsuccessfully challenged Bell's claim to be first. The controversy over who actually invented the telephone was long and bitter, but it was Bell's device that was widely adopted.

SHOCKING INVENTION

Antonio Meucci got the idea for a "speaking telegraph" in 1849 while using electricity to treat a man's migraine. The shock from the electrode in his mouth made the man cry out—and a copper wire carried the sound to Meucci, who was in the next room.

WIRELESS?

Like Edison's light bulb (see page 36), telephones would have been useless without a supporting web of wires. But here Bell had an advantage, for such a system already existed. Over the previous 35 years, a network of cables had spread across the world, carrying Morse code messages. The telephone replaced the electrical pulses of Morse with a voice signal. Over the next century, the early crackly phone calls grew clearer. Direct dialing and digital exchanges improved convenience and quality, and from 1915, the ability to call internationally made our world seem a dramatically smaller place. Even the first dial-up internet connections in the 1980s used a telephone network that had changed little since Bell's invention. It wasn't until the introduction of automatic cell phones in Japan in 1979 that we really ceased to rely on a thread of copper wire to hold a conversation with anyone out of earshot.

> ### CAN'T MANAGE WITHOUT IT?
> **People fear losing their phones almost as much as they fear a terrorist attack, according to a 2017 survey of 2,000 people by the Physiological Society.**

THE EVOLUTION OF THE
TELEPHONE

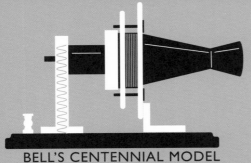

BELL'S CENTENNIAL MODEL
1876

FIRST COMMERCIAL TELEPHONE
1877

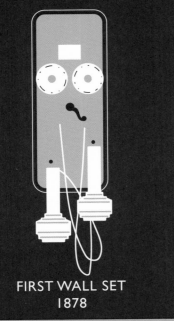

FIRST WALL SET
1878

FIRST
PUBLIC COIN PAY PHONE
1889

FIRST DESK SET
1892

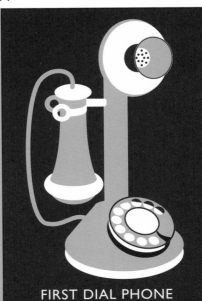

FIRST DIAL PHONE
1892

DESK SET TELEPHONE
1930s

MODEL 500 TELEPHONE
1949

PUSH-BUTTON PHONE
1960s

UHF RADIOTELEPHONE
1964

HANDHELD
CELLULAR PHONE
1973

CELL PHONE WITH
INTERNAL ANTENNA
1998

TOUCH SCREEN
SMARTPHONE
2002

ELECTRICITY

To nineteenth-century scientists, electricity was a novelty that could create sparks, heat, or movement. But making use of electricity meant inventing an industry to generate and distribute it.

ELECTRICITY IS SO MUCH a part of our lives that we barely notice it—until there is a power outage. Our computers, phones, stoves, and heat all go off, and at night we are plunged into complete darkness—a reminder that few electrical appliances have been more significant than the light bulb. Arc lamps, the very first electric lights, were too bright for anything but street lighting. Inventors searched for an electric light that could be used indoors, and the first to succeed was British inventor Joseph Swan. In 1878, he pumped the air out of a glass bulb enclosing a filament (thread) of burned cotton. Connecting electricity made the bulb glow brilliantly. Though the filament burned out after forty hours' use, Swan was granted a patent for the invention two years later.

SUCCESS OR FAILURE?
Edison rejected the concept of failure. When asked by a reporter why, after 10,000 experiments, he had failed to make a successful battery, he replied, "I have not failed once. I have succeeded in proving that those 10,000 ways will not work. When I have eliminated the ways that will not work, I will find the way that will work."

AN AMERICAN "WIZARD"

When Swan began experimenting with electric light, he had a competitor in Thomas Edison, who was already a celebrity inventor in the United States and had built the world's first research laboratory. Edison's large team searched for a better filament. After testing 6,000 different materials, they settled on charred bamboo, which glowed for 50 days and nights before popping. Edison won a patent in 1880, and Swan disputed it. Eventually the two men merged their interests and formed a joint company, Edison & Swan, to sell light bulbs.

ALL CREDIT TO HIM

So if Swan made the first bulbs, why is Edison famous as the inventor? Because he didn't just make light bulbs: he created the electrical industry. Bulbs need electricity to glow, but nobody made it or sold it. Swan's first customer, industrial magnate William Armstrong, had to dam a river and build a turbine to power his light bulbs. Unlike Swan, Edison manufactured and supplied everything that was needed to generate, distribute, and control electric power, from huge power plants to the smallest lamp holder. By 1885, the Edison Illuminating Company was generating power in New York City and five other towns.

The light bulb began the electrification of our world, but once homes and offices were connected, inventors soon found other uses for electric power. The development of small electric motors made fans possible in 1882 and electric sewing machines in 1889. The electric kettle and the toaster—simple applications of the heating effect of electricity—soon followed. Today, six out of every seven homes worldwide are hooked up to the power grid. Others use solar power or home generators to supply this invisible yet indispensable energy.

"Mr. Edison's efforts in electric lighting seem cursed with a total absence of originality."

THE *SATURDAY REVIEW* IN 1880

TAR AND TURTLES
Among the problems that plagued the first electric street lighting experiments were box turtles, which feasted on the tar insulation that protected the cables.

THE INCANDESCENT
LIGHT BULB

This diagram shows one of Edison's original bulbs, but for a century afterward light bulbs hardly changed. They were called *incandescent* because passing electricity through the thin filament made them incandesce — or glow white-hot.

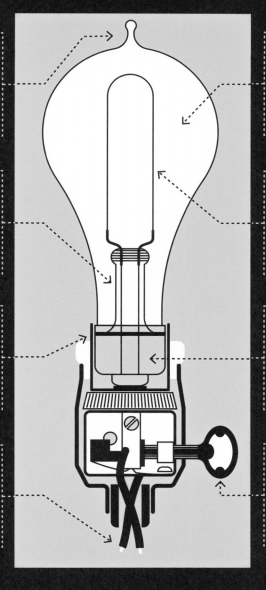

Glass globe
This fragile blip shows where the pump was attached to suck out the air.

Glass stem
The wires to provide power were fused into the glass tube that supported the filament.

Screw thread
Edison's design for the cap of the lamp remains unchanged to the present day.

Electrical wires
As the bulbs usually replaced a gas jet, the electrical wires were run along the existing gas pipes.

Vacuum
Oxygen inside the bulb would have allowed the filament to burn, so a special pump removed all but a hundred-millionth of the air.

Filament
A narrow strip of carbonized bamboo fiber provided the high electrical resistance that enabled the bulb to glow.

Insulation
The wires passed through an insulating filler that cemented the glass globe into the cap.

Switch
The bulb holder incorporated a circuit breaker to switch the light on and off.

Regular incandescent light bulbs are being phased out in many countries because they are inefficient: only one-tenth of the power they use produces light. The rest is wasted as heat. Newer kinds of bulbs use far less power and last much longer. They can reduce energy consumption dramatically.

TRADITIONAL INCANDESCENT	HALOGEN INCANDESCENT	COMPACT FLUORESCENT (CFL)	LIGHT-EMITTING DIODE (LED)

15 LUMENS PER WATT	25 LUMENS PER WATT	60 LUMENS PER WATT	72 LUMENS PER WATT
1,000 HOURS' BULB LIFE	3,000 HOURS' BULB LIFE	10,000 HOURS' BULB LIFE	25,000 HOURS' BULB LIFE

THE INTERNAL COMBUSTION ENGINE

Who would drive an explosion-powered car? Everyone, actually!
Deep inside the motors that keep most of our vehicles moving,
fuel and air burn with a "BANG!"—thousands of times a mile.

THE IDEA OF using explosions to power an engine is even older than the first steam engine (see page 28). Dutch physicist and clock inventor Christiaan Huygens tried to build an engine powered by gunpowder around 1678. It never worked properly, but Huygens got one thing right: he recognized that by burning fuel inside an engine—internal combustion—he could make the engine fast, efficient, and small. The first practical internal combustion engine was developed nearly two centuries later by German engineer Nikolaus Otto. Otto's engine burned a mixture of gas and air inside a metal cylinder sealed with a piston. As in a modern car engine, one explosion powered four strokes of the piston.

> "I believe in the horse. The automobile is only a temporary phenomenon."
>
> **GERMAN RULER KAISER WILHELM II IN 1905**

THE FIRST AUTOMOBILES

Otto built his engine in 1876 with help from engineers Gottlieb Daimler and Wilhelm Maybach, but their partnership didn't last. Jealous of Daimler's education, Otto fired him. Taking Maybach with him, Daimler began to work on engines of his own in his summerhouse. By 1885, they had built a gas-fueled engine small enough to fit in a vehicle, which they used to power a motorbike, the Reitwagen ("riding car" in German).

The four-wheeled vehicles that soon followed sparked a radical change in transportation. Called "horseless carriages," these early motor cars were noisy, slow, and unreliable, but they had one huge advantage over their four-legged competitors. Horses, which powered virtually all

STINKY PROBLEM
In New York in 1908, the internal combustion engine had yet to replace the city's 120,000 horses, each of which left about 22 pounds (10 kilograms) of solid waste on the streets daily. One journalist described this as "an economic burden, an affront to cleanliness, and a terrible tax upon human life."

other road transportation, fouled the streets with steaming, stinking piles. Horseless carriages promised to cleanse the cities of this very visible pollution—and they did.

FILTH IN THE AIR, NOT IN THE GUTTER

As we now know, the internal combustion engine did not really banish pollution. It simply exchanged one sort for another, filling the air with poisonous (though invisible) fumes. But until traffic growth made air pollution a problem, the internal combustion engine transformed our world. For those who could afford them, cars became symbols of individual freedom, providing fast personal transportation to remote places. Those who worked in cities could live far outside them, in greener suburbs. A luxury and a novelty at the start of the twentieth century, the car had become a necessity by the end. Today, the average American family owns two "horseless carriages."

RED FLAG MAN
Britain's lawmakers so feared motor vehicles that in 1865, they ruled that cars should travel no faster than 4 mph (6 kph), and that a man waving a red flag should walk 180 feet (55 meters) ahead. This Red Flag Act applied until 1896.

THE FOUR-STROKE ENGINE

To power a vehicle, the engine burns a mix of fuel and air. In four strokes (movements) the pistons each slide up and down twice, doing a different job at each stroke. The cycle of suck-squeeze-bang-blow repeats endlessly as the engine runs.

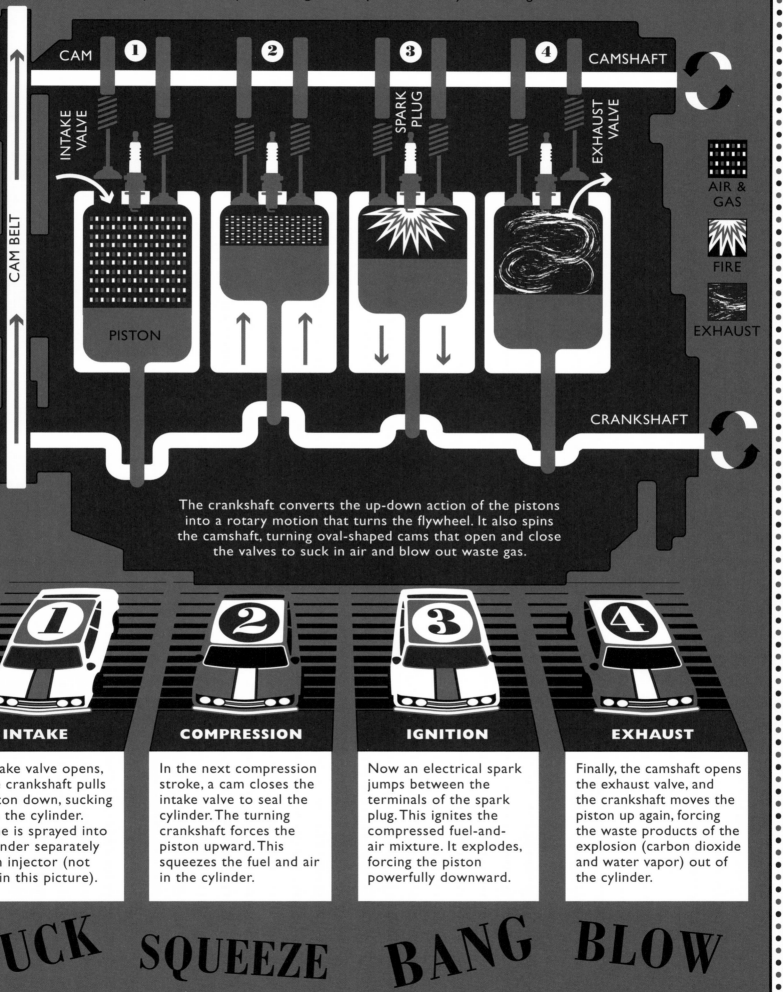

CAM ① ② ③ ④ CAMSHAFT

INTAKE VALVE

SPARK PLUG

EXHAUST VALVE

CAM BELT

PISTON

AIR & GAS

FIRE

EXHAUST

CRANKSHAFT

The crankshaft converts the up-down action of the pistons into a rotary motion that turns the flywheel. It also spins the camshaft, turning oval-shaped cams that open and close the valves to suck in air and blow out waste gas.

INTAKE

The intake valve opens, and the crankshaft pulls the piston down, sucking air into the cylinder. Gasoline is sprayed into the cylinder separately from an injector (not shown in this picture).

COMPRESSION

In the next compression stroke, a cam closes the intake valve to seal the cylinder. The turning crankshaft forces the piston upward. This squeezes the fuel and air in the cylinder.

IGNITION

Now an electrical spark jumps between the terminals of the spark plug. This ignites the compressed fuel-and-air mixture. It explodes, forcing the piston powerfully downward.

EXHAUST

Finally, the camshaft opens the exhaust valve, and the crankshaft moves the piston up again, forcing the waste products of the explosion (carbon dioxide and water vapor) out of the cylinder.

SUCK   SQUEEZE   BANG   BLOW

AVIATION

In the race to build the first flying machine, bat-like hang gliders battled ground-hugging, steam-powered monsters. The surprise winner was a powered kite with wings like a soaring buzzard, built by a pair of bicycle mechanics.

FLIGHT CONTROL
The Wright brothers guided *Flyer I* by twisting its wings to alter the flow of air over them— a mechanism Wilbur devised while fiddling restlessly with a bicycle inner tube box.

IN DECEMBER 1903, a couple of well-dressed men dragged a flimsy frame of wood, wire, and canvas across a windswept beach at Kitty Hawk, North Carolina. One of them climbed aboard while the other untied the rope that held the mechanism in place. As a roaring engine spun twin propellers, the primitive kite-like aircraft lumbered forward and gradually lifted off the ground. The plane stayed in the air for 12 seconds on its first flight before settling back onto the sand. It didn't seem like much to celebrate, but the feat thrilled and delighted the two brothers, Wilbur and Orville Wright. Their "flying machine" (quickly christened *Flyer I*) was the very first heavier-than-air powered aircraft to fly under the control of a pilot.

BEATING THE WORLD'S BEST

The pair's achievement was astonishing—for many reasons. They were complete amateurs, with no engineering training. They had beaten well-funded "experts" from around the world, spending barely $1,000 and dedicating four years of mostly part-time work to building and flying a series of increasingly sophisticated craft. And on the way to the world's first successful flight they had also invented the wind tunnel and the airplane propeller.

BIKE TEST
To check the lifting ability of different wing shapes, the brothers bolted an ingenious testing rig to the front of a bike. To simulate the airflow of flight, they pedaled furiously through the streets of their hometown, Dayton, Ohio.

THE FLIGHT THAT MADE THE WORLD SMALLER

Today's sleek passenger aircraft look very different from the Wrights' flimsy *Flyer I*, whose very first flight would not even have cleared the length of a jumbo jet. But all of modern aviation has grown out of Wilbur and Orville's vision and ingenuity. Just 10 years after that historic moment at Kitty Hawk, the first regular passenger air service began between two Florida towns. Thirty-five years later, in 1939, the first jet aircraft flew, heralding a new era in rapid air travel—and warfare. Seventy years later, the world's fastest aircraft flew nearly 7 miles (11 kilometers) in the same amount of time that Wilbur Wright had been airborne on that first historic flight. Now, thanks to powerful jet engines, aircraft can reach anywhere in the world in a day or less—and airline passengers together fly 13 billion miles (21 billion kilometers) every day.

> **"They done it! They done it! Damned if they ain't flew!"**
> **A LIFEBOATMAN WHO WITNESSED THE FLIGHT IN 1903**

The JET ENGINE

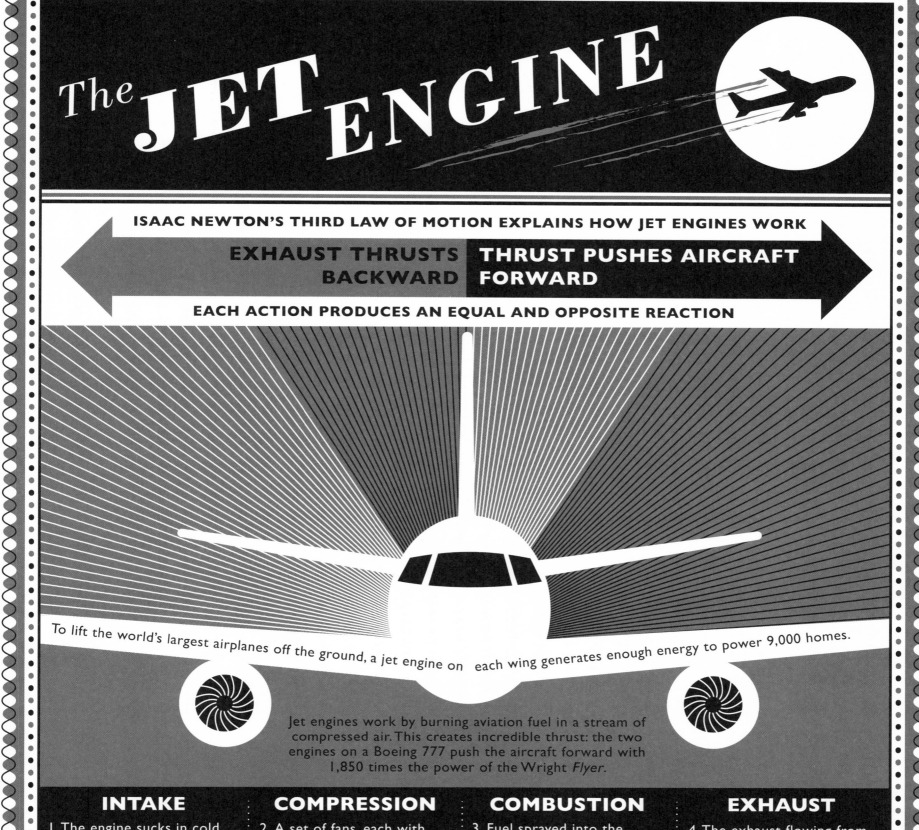

ISAAC NEWTON'S THIRD LAW OF MOTION EXPLAINS HOW JET ENGINES WORK

← EXHAUST THRUSTS BACKWARD

THRUST PUSHES AIRCRAFT FORWARD →

EACH ACTION PRODUCES AN EQUAL AND OPPOSITE REACTION

To lift the world's largest airplanes off the ground, a jet engine on each wing generates enough energy to power 9,000 homes.

Jet engines work by burning aviation fuel in a stream of compressed air. This creates incredible thrust: the two engines on a Boeing 777 push the aircraft forward with 1,850 times the power of the Wright *Flyer*.

INTAKE
1. The engine sucks in cold air at the front. The intake is carefully shaped so that air flows in smoothly.

COMPRESSION
2. A set of fans, each with many blades, compresses (squeezes) the air flowing into the engine.

COMBUSTION
3. Fuel sprayed into the engine mixes with the compressed air and burns furiously, creating power.

EXHAUST
4. The exhaust flowing from the engine provides thrust and turns a turbine powering the compressor.

AIR INTAKE

EXHAUST

FUEL BURNER — COMBUSTION CHAMBER

RADIO

First demonstrated as "wireless telegraphy" by an ingenious young Italian in 1896, radio has shaped our world, giving us almost magical powers of control and communication.

THE SON OF a wealthy Italian landowner, Guglielmo Marconi was fascinated by Hertzian waves. Generated by electric sparks, these invisible rays could be detected some distance away. The waves were named for Heinrich Hertz, who had discovered them a decade earlier but failed to recognize their value. Young Marconi, however, did. He guessed that Hertzian waves could carry messages through thin air and around obstacles. They would be especially valuable, he reasoned, where a telegraph cable would not work—to contact ships at sea, for example.

WAVE AFTER WAVE

In the loft of his family mansion, Marconi repeated Hertz's experiments and those of other scientists who had studied what we now call radio waves. He first built a machine to make sparks, then bent a metal wire into a circle, leaving a small gap. When his machine created a spark, a second spark jumped across the gap in the ring. In 1895, Marconi created aerials, and a receiver more sensitive than a metal ring. His butler, Mignani, carried the receiver into the garden, waving a handkerchief to signal the reception of Marconi's sparks. Then he went to the top of Celestini Hill, a mile away, and could receive the transmissions there.

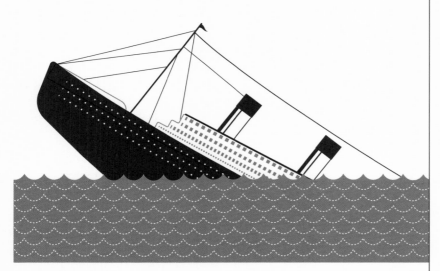

RADIO RESCUE
Radio received a big boost when the "unsinkable" ocean liner *Titanic* was punctured by an Atlantic iceberg in 1912. The ship had a Marconi wireless, and the radio operators used it to summon help, saving more than 700 lives. Following the disaster, international rules forced all ships to install radios.

When Mignani disappeared out of sight beyond the hill, a "bang!" from his hunting rifle signaled success.

To exploit his device, Marconi—who was then only twenty-one years old—traveled to Britain. His family had contacts there, and, as he put it, Britain had a "large fleet . . . and large shipping interests." In London, a senior official at the Post Office arranged for him to demonstrate his apparatus. In May 1897, he transmitted the first radio message 3 miles (5 kilometers) across the sea. By 1901, he had succeeded in sending the letter *S* in Morse code across the Atlantic Ocean.

IS IT MAGIC?
Marconi's demonstrations seemed so miraculous that people searched for the wires linking transmitter and receiver. Newspaper stories described him as a wizard and compared him to escapologist Harry Houdini, who was wildly popular at the time.

WIRELESS TELEGRAPHY

Marconi patented "wireless telegraphy" and quickly turned his apparatus into transmitters and receivers he could sell. They sent signals only in Morse code, but by 1906, voice broadcasts had begun.

Today we rely on a blizzard of radio waves. Radio signals reach beyond our solar system, controlling spacecraft 12 billion miles (20 billion kilometers) away. And they help us at the closest distances, sending details from a credit card to a cash register just centimeters away. Marconi's once-exotic vision of silent, invisible airborne messages has grown into an essential way of doing almost anything without wires.

"It is of no use whatsoever. This is just an experiment. . . . We just have these mysterious electromagnetic waves that we cannot see with the naked eye."

SCIENTIST HEINRICH HERTZ DISMISSES STUDENTS' SUGGESTIONS THAT RADIO WAVES MIGHT BE USEFUL, IN 1888

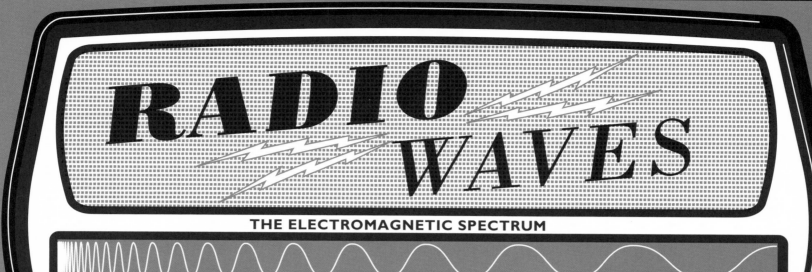

RADIO WAVES

THE ELECTROMAGNETIC SPECTRUM

GAMMA RAYS X-RAYS ULTRAVIOLET VISIBLE INFRARED MICROWAVES RADIO WAVES

 Radio waves are just part of the electromagnetic spectrum, which also includes visible light, infrared and ultraviolet radiation, and X-rays. The properties of each type of radiation depend on its wavelength — the distance between successive peaks of energy.

Aside from the lowest frequencies, there is a use for every part of the radio spectrum. The lower the frequency, the greater the ability of a radio wave to penetrate obstacles. For example, ELF radio can pass through seawater, so it can be used to communicate with distant submarines. By contrast, a clear line-of-sight path between the transmitter and receiver is optimal for a UHF broadcast. Higher frequencies are useful where a short range is an advantage, such as for contactless credit cards.

BAND	WAVELENGTH	FREQUENCY	HUMAN USE
Extremely low frequency — ELF	100,000–10,000 km	3–30 Hz	Submarine communication
Super low frequency — SLF	10,000–1,000 km	30–300 Hz	Submarine communication
Ultra low frequency — ULF	1,000–100 km	300–3,000 Hz	Ground-penetrating radio broadcasts in mines
Very low frequency — VLF	100–10 km	3–30 kHz	Time signals, submarines
Low frequency — LF	10–1 km	30–300 kHz	Long-wave broadcasts, navigation beacons
Medium frequency — MF	1000–100 m	300–3,000 kHz	Medium-wave broadcasts (AM radio)
High frequency — HF	100–10 m	3–30 MHz	Shortwave broadcasts
Very high frequency — VHF	10–1 m	30–300 MHz	FM radio, TV, air traffic control
Ultra high frequency — UHF	100–10 cm	300–3,000 MHz	TV, cell phones, Wi-Fi, Bluetooth
Super high frequency — SHF	100–10 mm	3–30 GHz	Radar, microwave communication
Extremely high frequency — EHF	10–1 mm	30–300 GHz	Missile tracking, security scanning
Tremendously high frequency — THF	1–0.1 mm	300–3,000 GHz	Medical imaging, security scanning

Shortwave radio signals bounce off a layer of the atmosphere called the ionosphere, so they travel farther. Reflection is stronger at night, when it is possible to tune in to stations all over the world.

Communications satellites orbit beyond the ionosphere, which does not reflect the high-frequency radio signals used for satellite communications.

IONOSPHERE

EARTH

FILM & TELEVISION

It took a combination of eccentricity, improvisation, and creative genius to bring photographs to life on movie and TV screens.

THE INVENTION OF PHOTOGRAPHY in 1838 suggested an intriguing possibility: what if these lifelike images could move? It remained just a dream until, nearly 40 years later, a wealthy Californian wanted to know whether a horse took all its hooves off the ground when trotting. Horse breeder Leland Stanford hired photographer Eadweard Muybridge to prove that it did. Muybridge rigged a dozen cameras, triggered them with trip wires, and made the world's first animated action sequence—of an airborne horse.

> "Go down to reception and get rid of the lunatic who's down there. He says he's got a machine for seeing by wireless."
>
> **THE NEWS EDITOR OF THE LONDON *DAILY EXPRESS* REFUSES TO SEE TV INVENTOR BAIRD IN 1925**

FLICKERING PEEP SHOWS

A one-second sequence is hardly a movie, however, and a succession of inventors struggled to do better. William Dickson may not have been the first to succeed when he built his Kinetograph camera in 1891, but the power of his employer, Thomas Edison, ensured that his were the first movies to be widely exhibited. These early silent films were seen by one person at a time in Kinetoscope peep shows. The experience of sitting with others in a movie theater began only when French brothers Auguste and Louis Lumière devised a projector in 1895.

LOW BUDGET OR NO BUDGET?
The movies that make Hollywood great cost millions: *Pirates of the Caribbean: On Stranger Tides* holds the record at $378 million. But you no longer need a huge budget to make films. High-quality video cameras are cheap, and you can edit movies on a home computer—or simply use the phone in your pocket. You could be the next Steven Spielberg!

INVENTING THE TV

The Lumières' movie shows coincided with the first experiments in radio, and in 1926, Scottish inventor John Logie Baird brought these two technologies together to broadcast moving pictures. The first television system was built from a hatbox, sealing wax, darning needles, and bicycle lights … but it worked! Baird's makeshift TV system was improved by the BBC, but by 1937, it was clear that it would never be popular:

the screens were too small and the pictures fuzzy. In its place, broadcasters adopted an electronic system devised by an inventive American farm boy, Philo Farnsworth, who had the idea when harrowing a field at age fourteen. The neat parallel lines cut in the soil inspired him to use an electronic scanning system for both a camera and a TV set. Eventually adopted by major electronic companies, Farnsworth's "image dissector" was developed into the TV system that endured until the introduction of digital TV around the year 2000.

By then, TV had revolutionized news and entertainment, bringing the world—and a world of performance—into every living room. Expanded by cable services, VCRs, and home videos, TV was the public's favorite way to relax. Even today, with a limitless choice of media available, many of us still choose to flop in front of the television at the end of a hard day.

GHOULISH TV
Faced with the limitations of his spinning-disk camera, Baird tried using a human eye to record TV images. A surgeon gave him a spare eyeball, and Baird rushed it to his laboratory. The experiment failed, as Baird recorded in his journal: "On the following day the sensitiveness of the eye's visual nerve was gone."

MOVING IMAGES

A set of images from Muybridge's *Horse in Motion* series

SPINNING CYLINDER

SLITS

SPINNING CYLINDER

LINE OF SIGHT

Movie pioneer Eadweard Muybridge had no projector, so he brought his galloping horse sequence to life on a simple toy, the zoetrope. It was little more than a cake pan with viewing slots cut in the sides. Spinning the pan and looking through the slots, a viewer saw the picture sequence pasted inside. Flickering past, and displayed only briefly, the images merged together, giving an illusion of a smoothly moving horse.

REFRIGERATION

Imagine a world where fresh food rots in days, where medicines must be used as soon as they are made, and where summer's heat is deadly. That's a world without refrigeration.

CHILLING IS NOT A MODERN OBSESSION—in China, people tried it 3,000 years ago. In winter they cut ice from flooded fields, protecting it from heat to use in summer. The poem "Seventh Month," from a famous collection called *The Book of Songs,* describes how "In the second month after midwinter we chop river ice with cold blows. In the third, store the slabs in the dark of the icehouse."

Chinese people probably didn't use the ice for preserving food. Almost all early use of ice—in Palestine, Egypt, Greece, and Italy—was for chilling drinks. Thirst, it seems, beats hunger.

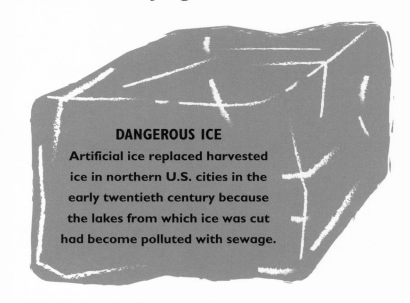

DANGEROUS ICE
Artificial ice replaced harvested ice in northern U.S. cities in the early twentieth century because the lakes from which ice was cut had become polluted with sewage.

MAKING ICE

Harvested ice has drawbacks: it slowly melts, and when it's gone, there won't be more until the next winter. Ice lovers have therefore always looked for ways to make it wherever and whenever they want. In 1758, Benjamin Franklin and British chemist John Hadley froze water by using a bellows to evaporate ether—a chemical that cools quickly when it turns to vapor. Although they did not try to build a refrigerator, the result of their experiment was much like what happens in fridges and freezers today: heat was absorbed by turning a liquid to a vapor. But making a practical cooler also means unwinding this process: turning the vapor back into a liquid and shedding the heat it releases. By about 1850, inventors had overcome this hurdle, creating devices that reliably made ice.

> "One may see the possibility of freezing a man to death on a warm summer's day."
>
> **BENJAMIN FRANKLIN, AFTER MAKING ICE ARTIFICIALLY IN 1758**

ESSENTIAL COOLING

This was only the beginning of refrigeration. Cooling has achieved much more than just making drinks refreshing. Low temperatures keep food fresh on its way from harvest to kitchen, making it possible to farm more remote regions; and without cooling, many life-saving vaccines would spoil before they can be injected. The development of air-conditioning has made buildings more comfortable in hot climates and changed where people can live, making possible desert cities that would otherwise be almost unbearable in the summer.

Early refrigeration systems were built for the factory, ship, or railroad car and were big and clumsy. It wasn't until the twentieth century that the first household refrigerators appeared, and they were expensive: in 1927, the General Electric Monitor Top cost five weeks' wages for a construction worker. Today, fridges are no longer a luxury, and fewer than one in a hundred homes lack them.

CITY HERDS

Without refrigeration, milk turns sour even on short road journeys. In the nineteenth century, cow herds in city-center barns provided neighborhood milk supplies. Twenty thousand milk cows lived in central London in 1854; in New York there were 2,000 in Brooklyn alone.

THE WORKINGS OF A
FRIDGE

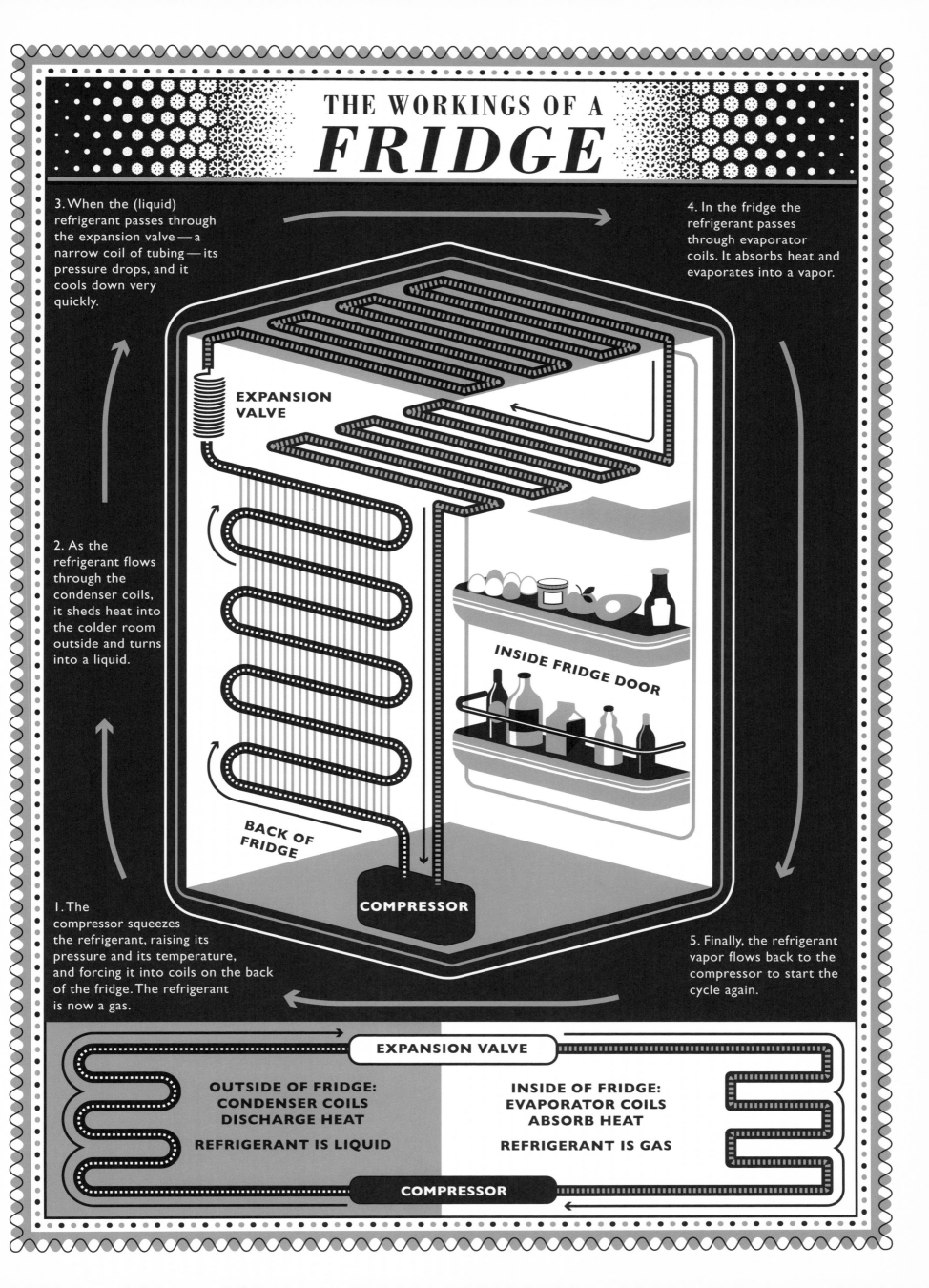

3. When the (liquid) refrigerant passes through the expansion valve — a narrow coil of tubing — its pressure drops, and it cools down very quickly.

4. In the fridge the refrigerant passes through evaporator coils. It absorbs heat and evaporates into a vapor.

EXPANSION VALVE

2. As the refrigerant flows through the condenser coils, it sheds heat into the colder room outside and turns into a liquid.

INSIDE FRIDGE DOOR

BACK OF FRIDGE

1. The compressor squeezes the refrigerant, raising its pressure and its temperature, and forcing it into coils on the back of the fridge. The refrigerant is now a gas.

COMPRESSOR

5. Finally, the refrigerant vapor flows back to the compressor to start the cycle again.

EXPANSION VALVE

OUTSIDE OF FRIDGE: CONDENSER COILS DISCHARGE HEAT

REFRIGERANT IS LIQUID

INSIDE OF FRIDGE: EVAPORATOR COILS ABSORB HEAT

REFRIGERANT IS GAS

COMPRESSOR

ANTIBIOTICS

An untidy laboratory led to the discovery of a potent bacteria-killing mold, but its importance wasn't recognized until there was an urgent need for lifesaving drugs in a world torn apart by war.

WHEN SCOTTISH SCIENTIST Alexander Fleming returned from vacation in 1928, his laboratory at St Mary's Hospital in London was a mess. Cleaning up, he noticed something odd in a glass petri dish. Furry islands of bacteria were growing in the nutrient jelly it contained. But a fleck of mold had drifted into the center and killed a surrounding circle of bacteria. The mold was a natural antibiotic. Fleming did some experiments and found that the mold's active ingredient, which he called penicillin, killed bacteria even when diluted 500 times. He wrote a journal article suggesting that penicillin might make a good disinfectant; it was ignored. He gave a lecture; his audience was uninterested. Fleming was a busy man, and he put aside his discovery.

A WOUNDED WORLD

Fleming's work might have been forgotten if not for World War II. Australian Howard Florey, a professor of pathology at Oxford University, realized that antibiotics could save the lives of fighters whose wounds became infected. He recruited biochemist Ernst Chain, a Jewish refugee from Nazi Germany, and had him read scientific papers. Chain found Fleming's paper and, with Florey and several other scientists, began building on his work. In February 1941, they tested a tiny sample of the drug on a policeman who was dying of a bacterial infection. He improved, but the penicillin quickly ran out. Without its protection, the man died.

NOBEL PRIZE
In 1945, Fleming, Florey, and Chain shared the Nobel Prize in Medicine for their discovery. However, Fleming received by far the most attention and publicity—perhaps because his "lucky accident" story was easily understood and more inspiring than the hard work of the other two.

"Superbugs are gaining strength because we continue to squander these precious medicines . . . as cheap production tools in animal agriculture."

LANCE PRICE, AN ANTIBIOTIC RESEARCHER AT GEORGE WASHINGTON UNIVERSITY IN WASHINGTON, DC, IN 2017

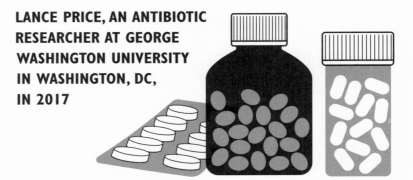

MAKING IT

This human trial proved the effectiveness of penicillin, but manufacturing it in large quantities was a bigger challenge. The problem was solved only when the United States government realized the importance of the drug and poured huge resources into its development. Researchers found ways to make the lifesaving mold grow more quickly and to purify it in large quantities. By the end of the World War II, U.S. factories were producing 650 billion doses a month.

Since the discovery of penicillin, antibiotics have been our most powerful weapon for fighting bacteria. Without antibiotics, treatments such as organ transplants would be impossible. However, you can have too much of a good thing. Today farmers add antibiotics to animal feed to speed growth, and doctors prescribe the drugs for viral infections that antibiotics cannot cure. This casual use has allowed many deadly "superbugs" to become immune to antibiotics. We are in danger of returning to a time when a simple scratch could be deadly.

MOLDY MELONS
In the 1940s, scientists in Peoria, Illinois, were hoping to find a strain of the mold that was more efficient at producing the lifesaving chemical. They sampled soil from all over the world, but the best source turned out to be a moldy cantaloupe bought in a local fruit market.

HOW ANTIBIOTICS WORK

Antibiotics attack bacteria—but must not harm human cells. They do this in one of two ways: by stopping processes that take place only in bacteria and not in their human host, or by targeting parts of a bacteria cell, such as the wall, that human cells don't have.

Antibiotics can target bacterial reproduction.

Antibiotics can target bacterial protein synthesis.

Antibiotics can target bacterial cell wall synthesis.

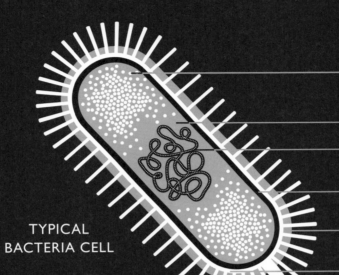

TYPICAL BACTERIA CELL

RIBOSOMES

CYTOPLASM

DNA

PLASMA MEMBRANE

CAPSULE

CELL WALL

FIMBRIAE

BACTERIAL FLAGELLUM

ANTIBIOTIC RESISTANCE

1. Small numbers of bacteria evolve a natural resistance to the antibiotic because they have a mutation (a change in DNA).

2. A dose of the antibiotic kills off ordinary bacteria, but the drug-resistant ones survive the medication and begin to multiply.

3. Treating new infections with the same antibiotic wipes out the ordinary bacteria, leaving only the resistant ones.

4. Once the drug-resistant bacteria outnumber the ordinary bacteria, the antibiotic can no longer control the infection.

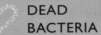 LIVE BACTERIA

 DEAD BACTERIA

 DRUG-RESISTANT BACTERIA

DRUG-RESISTANT BACTERIA MUTANT

WIDESPREAD ANTIBIOTIC RESISTANCE

Farmers feed antibiotics to animals as a protection against infection when they are not always needed.

Bacteria develop resistance to antibiotics, then infect humans through the food chain.

Doctors sometimes prescribe antibiotics when they are not needed, leading to more bacteria being exposed to antibiotics and developing resistance.

Resistant infections spread, and antibiotics no longer cure them.

NUCLEAR FISSION

If we could completely convert just 25 ounces (700 grams) of any matter—uranium, marmalade, toenail clippings—into energy, it would provide all the power the world needs for one hour.

IF THERE IS ONE equation that everyone knows, it is $E = mc^2$. This is Albert Einstein's 1905 proposal that matter (m) and energy (E) are one and the same. The c in the equation is the speed of light: 186,000 miles (300,000 kilometers) a second. Squaring c (that is, multiplying it by itself) makes an unimaginably big number, so very little matter creates an awful lot of energy.

In practice, turning matter directly into energy is not possible, but c^2 is so huge that by splitting atoms into smaller parts and annihilating just a tiny amount of their mass, we still get a lot of power. This is called nuclear fission.

A BIG BANG

Nuclear fission was first demonstrated in 1938 by German chemist Otto Hahn. When word of his experiment spread, scientists in Europe and the USA realized that, using the right nuclear fuels, they could create a runaway chain reaction. They could choose to use nuclear energy peacefully, to generate very cheap electricity, or for military might—as a massively powerful explosive. When World War II broke out in 1939, scientists in the United States began working to create an atom bomb. The Manhattan Project, as it was called, grew to employ nearly 130,000 people in the USA, Canada, and Britain. At enormous cost, the scientists and engineers produced enough plutonium and uranium fuel to test a bomb ("the Gadget") and then drop two more on the Japanese cities of Hiroshima and Nagasaki, killing between 130,000 and 226,000 people. The consequences of these attacks were so horrifying that nuclear weapons have never been used since.

CHIEF OF THE BOMB
When he watched the first nuclear bomb test in 1945, J. Robert Oppenheimer, scientific director of the Manhattan Project, commented simply, "It worked!" But later he hinted at his regrets, quoting a sacred Hindu text: *"Now I am become Death, the destroyer of worlds."*

"A tablet of atomic fuel no larger than a vitamin pill will be enough to operate your automobile for a year."

PULITZER PRIZE–WINNING JOURNALIST DAVID DIETZ PREDICTS ABUNDANT NUCLEAR POWER IN 1962

EVEN MORE ENERGY
Nuclear fusion (merging atoms to form heavier ones) keeps our sun glowing. If we could repeat the trick on Earth, it would provide unlimited power without the hazards of nuclear fission. Unfortunately, building a working fusion reactor has proved impossible so far. Physicists joke that fusion power is just 30 years away—and always will be.

CIVILIAN POWER

After the war, work began on peaceful uses for nuclear fission, and to begin with, the results were promising. In 1951, the first experimental nuclear power plant generated electricity, and three years later, U.S. Atomic Energy Commission chairman Lewis Strauss asserted that nuclear power plants could in the future deliver electricity that would be "too cheap to meter." This never happened, but for countries that lacked fossil fuels, nuclear power plants provided reliable energy without oil or oil imports. In France, for example, four out of every five houses run on nuclear-generated power.

Elsewhere the nuclear promise has not been fulfilled. The nuclear industry has suffered from high costs and terrible accidents. Disposing of radioactive nuclear waste remains an unsolved problem. Though nuclear power produces about a tenth of the world's electricity today, wind and solar are cheaper, cleaner sources of power.

NUCLEAR REACTOR

A nuclear power plant uses the heat produced by nuclear fission reactions to turn water into steam, which spins turbines, generating electricity. Within the reactor, control rods regulate power production by absorbing the neutrons that keep the chain reaction running.

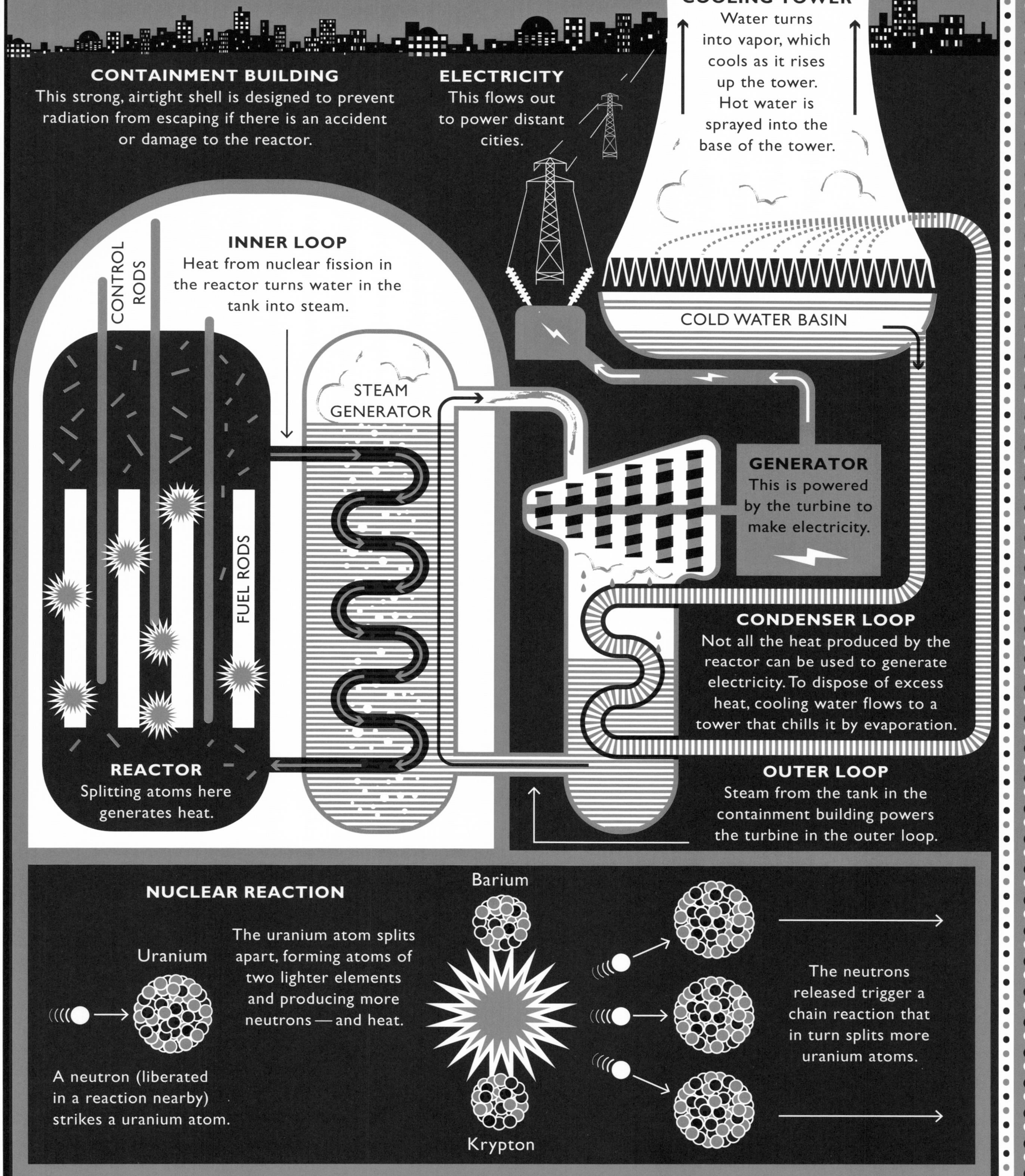

CONTAINMENT BUILDING
This strong, airtight shell is designed to prevent radiation from escaping if there is an accident or damage to the reactor.

ELECTRICITY
This flows out to power distant cities.

COOLING TOWER
Water turns into vapor, which cools as it rises up the tower. Hot water is sprayed into the base of the tower.

COLD WATER BASIN

INNER LOOP
Heat from nuclear fission in the reactor turns water in the tank into steam.

CONTROL RODS

STEAM GENERATOR

FUEL RODS

GENERATOR
This is powered by the turbine to make electricity.

CONDENSER LOOP
Not all the heat produced by the reactor can be used to generate electricity. To dispose of excess heat, cooling water flows to a tower that chills it by evaporation.

REACTOR
Splitting atoms here generates heat.

OUTER LOOP
Steam from the tank in the containment building powers the turbine in the outer loop.

NUCLEAR REACTION

Uranium

A neutron (liberated in a reaction nearby) strikes a uranium atom.

The uranium atom splits apart, forming atoms of two lighter elements and producing more neutrons — and heat.

Barium

Krypton

The neutrons released trigger a chain reaction that in turn splits more uranium atoms.

SATELLITES

Since the first satellite was launched, some 60 years ago, we have come to rely on these shiny hunks of technology circling above us for everything from driving directions to time checks.

WHO INVENTED SATELLITES? English mathematician and scientist Isaac Newton didn't, but he was smart enough to predict them. In a famous 1687 thought experiment, he suggested firing a cannon from a mountaintop: a fast-enough cannonball, he reasoned, would never fall to Earth. Instead, it would climb high enough in the sky to partly escape gravity. At just the right speed and altitude, the earth's pull would exactly balance the ball's tendency to travel in a straight line and stop it from flying off into space. The cannonball would become a satellite, endlessly orbiting.

Newton used his imaginary satellite to explain about gravity in his famous book *A Treatise of the System of the World.* Unfortunately, he was not able to test his idea: even the most powerful cannon of his time had only a twentieth of the power needed to send a shell into orbit.

BLEEPING BALL

The first successful attempt to launch a satellite came three centuries later, when the Soviet Union (now Russia and fourteen neighboring countries) launched *Sputnik.* The size and shape of an exercise ball and made of polished metal, *Sputnik* rode into space atop a rocket in October 1957, transmitting simple radio tones.

WASTE IN SPACE

Not all satellites are useful. Thousands of redundant ones are still up there, posing a collision risk to new craft. Smaller space junk is a problem, too: there are at least 170 million bits bigger than 1 mm. Even the urine and feces discarded by 1960s astronauts remain a threat. Orbiting at 7,000 mph (11,000 kph), a lump of human waste the size of a plum has the same energy as a small car moving at highway speed.

DEATH FROM SPACE?

Sputnik's regular "beep-beep-beeps" were hardly a threat, but American newspapers used them to suggest that the Soviet Union had plans for sinister space weapons. These dire predictions of death from space did not come true. Although one of the earliest uses of the satellite was as an electronic spy gazing down at the armies and navies

"A hunk of iron almost anybody could launch."

US CHIEF OF NAVAL OPERATIONS RAWSON BENNETT DISMISSES THE LAUNCH OF *SPUTNIK* IN A TV INTERVIEW ON OCTOBER 4, 1957

of rival nations, most applications have been peaceable. Of the 1,500 or so working satellites still orbiting, only a quarter are military: far more provide services that we find indispensable. They guide us on journeys (see opposite); they beam down TV programs; they relay phone calls to remote places (see page 60 for more on communications satellites); they help us forecast the weather and harvests; and they monitor environmental destruction. But perhaps their most essential job is as super-accurate timekeepers: by synchronizing clocks on the ground, satellites keep the internet running, traffic moving, and banks and stock exchanges open. We'd literally be lost without them.

TRUTH OR FICTION?

A satellite 22,000 miles (35,900 kilometers) above the equator orbits exactly once a day, so it appears to stay in the same place in the sky. This "geostationary" orbit is a favorite place to park communications satellites—an idea popularized twelve years before *Sputnik* by science-fiction writer Arthur C. Clarke.

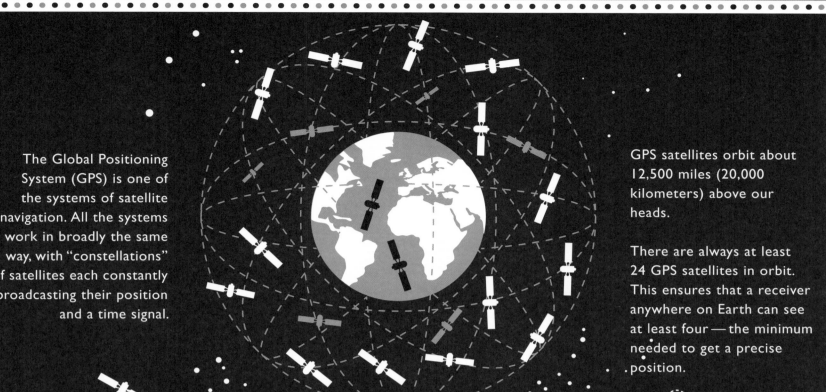

The Global Positioning System (GPS) is one of the systems of satellite navigation. All the systems work in broadly the same way, with "constellations" of satellites each constantly broadcasting their position and a time signal.

GPS satellites orbit about 12,500 miles (20,000 kilometers) above our heads.

There are always at least 24 GPS satellites in orbit. This ensures that a receiver anywhere on Earth can see at least four — the minimum needed to get a precise position.

SATELLITE NAVIGATION

Each satellite has a super-accurate clock, which is essential for checking its precise position. The satellites synchronize their clocks with one another, and with ground stations, every day.

Ground stations constantly check the satellites and take faulty ones out of service.

GPS receivers calculate where they are on Earth by timing the arrival of signals from four satellites. Clever calculations pinpoint positions to within 16 feet (5 meters).

The satellite navigation unit on a car dashboard has a comprehensive map stored in its memory. By using position information received from satellites, the unit can display the vehicle's position on the map.

TAKE SECOND RIGHT IN 0.5 MILES

Software in satellite navigation receivers allows you to set a destination and get turn-by-turn directions. Phones can pick up GPS signals, too, but they rely on the internet for map data, making them unreliable in remote places with no cellular data signal.

DNA

An American and a British scientist hurried into a Cambridge pub at the end of February 1953. Jubilantly and loudly, they announced that they had discovered "the secret of life."

JAMES WATSON and Francis Crick were young, cocky, and inexperienced, but theirs wasn't an idle boast. They had indeed revealed the structure of deoxyribonucleic acid, or DNA. Scientists had begun to suspect two years earlier that this thread-like molecule, found coiled in the cells of every plant and animal, worked like a template for all life. But Watson and Crick turned suspicion into certainty. They showed that DNA was double-helix shaped—that is, a spiral of paired molecules that was itself wrapped into a spiral. This staggering discovery had the potential to unlock the secret of human identity and the causes—and cures—of inherited disease.

DNA, CRIME, AND IDENTIFICATION

Only identical twins share the same DNA, and in 1984, British genetics professor Alec Jeffreys suddenly realized that DNA analysis could identify people uniquely. Today, matching DNA found at crime scenes with samples taken from suspects is a powerful way to solve crime and prove guilt.

PICTURING THE STRUCTURE

Watson had an unusual ability to picture in his mind complex molecular structures, but the key that unlocked the secret of DNA for him was a photograph of it taken by Rosalind Franklin, a rival in the race to find the molecule's structure. Franklin's "Photo 51" was taken not with a camera but using X-rays. It may have appeared to be a blurry pattern of blobs, but to Watson and Crick it could only have been created by a double helix. Franklin's colleague Maurice Wilkins showed Watson the picture

DIY DNA

What is DNA actually like? You can touch its gloopy strands by extracting it from strawberry pulp in your own kitchen. You can find details on the internet, but the basic experiment is simple: adding dishwashing liquid opens up the cells; adding salt makes the DNA clump together; filtering, and pouring in chilled rubbing alcohol, makes the DNA separate out.

"The best home for a feminist was in another person's lab."

JAMES WATSON, COMMENTING ON ROSALIND FRANKLIN IN 1968

without asking her permission and—at a time when sexism was common in laboratories—did not tell her that he had shared her discovery.

Aided by Photo 51, Crick and Watson were able to build a model of the molecule, and in April 1953, they published their findings in the science journal *Nature*.

MOLECULAR BIOLOGY

It was a sensational breakthrough: the discovery of DNA's structure provided a huge boost to the field of molecular biology—that is, the study of living things based on the arrangements of their individual chemicals. From Watson and Crick's work grew the modern science of genetics. This research has made it easier to solve crimes by analyzing DNA, to modify plant and animal breeds, and to personalize medical treatment for each patient. It has even made possible a "map" of the human genome—a diagram of which characteristics we all share, and which make us each unique.

In 1962, Watson, Crick, and Wilkins received for their work a Nobel Prize: science's richest award. Franklin had died of ovarian cancer four years earlier and was not given the award posthumously. It was a cruel irony, since gene research is now a vital tool in the search for cancer cures.

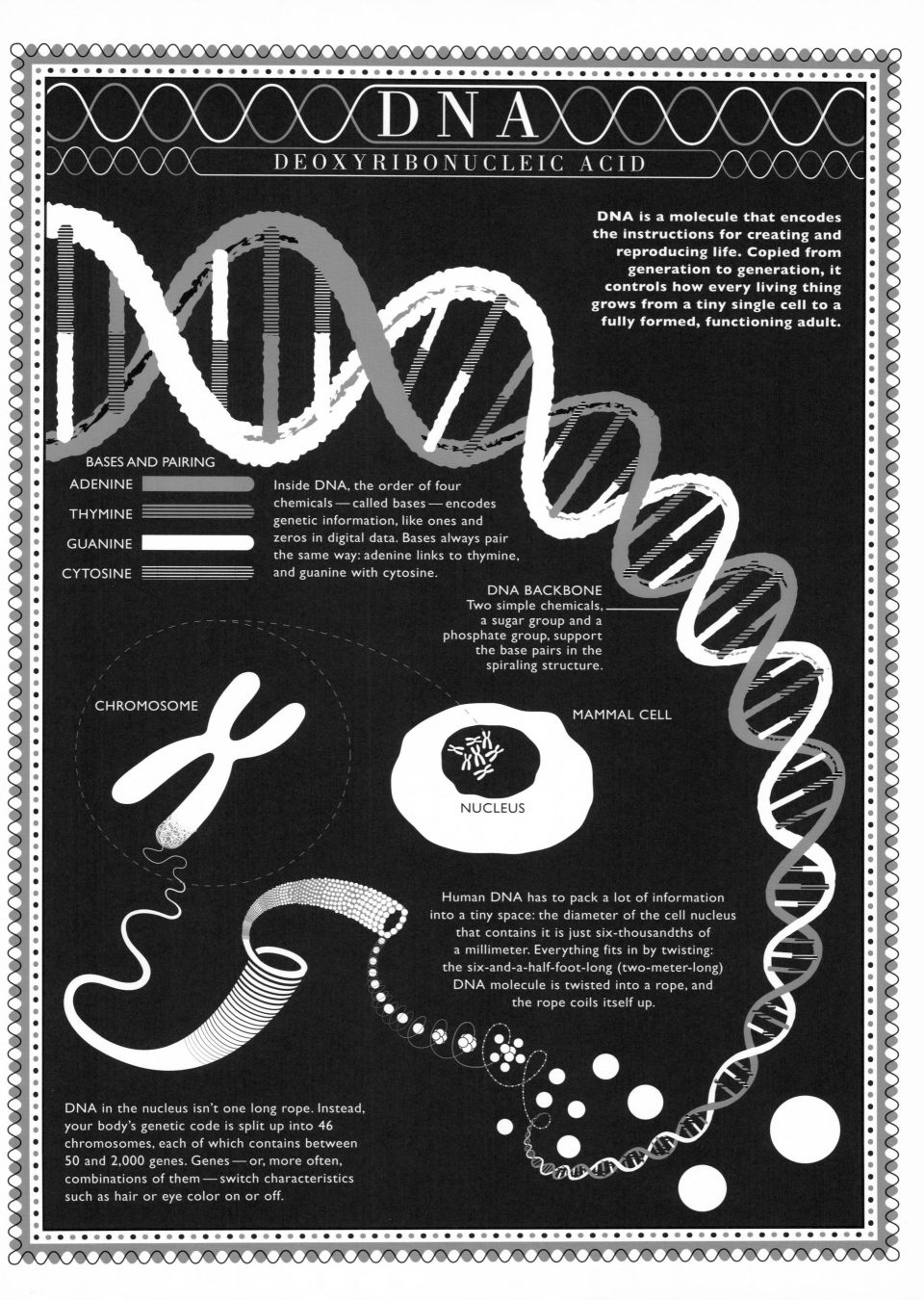

D N A

DEOXYRIBONUCLEIC ACID

DNA is a molecule that encodes the instructions for creating and reproducing life. Copied from generation to generation, it controls how every living thing grows from a tiny single cell to a fully formed, functioning adult.

BASES AND PAIRING

ADENINE

THYMINE

GUANINE

CYTOSINE

Inside DNA, the order of four chemicals — called bases — encodes genetic information, like ones and zeros in digital data. Bases always pair the same way: adenine links to thymine, and guanine with cytosine.

DNA BACKBONE
Two simple chemicals, a sugar group and a phosphate group, support the base pairs in the spiraling structure.

CHROMOSOME

MAMMAL CELL

NUCLEUS

Human DNA has to pack a lot of information into a tiny space: the diameter of the cell nucleus that contains it is just six-thousandths of a millimeter. Everything fits in by twisting: the six-and-a-half-foot-long (two-meter-long) DNA molecule is twisted into a rope, and the rope coils itself up.

DNA in the nucleus isn't one long rope. Instead, your body's genetic code is split up into 46 chromosomes, each of which contains between 50 and 2,000 genes. Genes — or, more often, combinations of them — switch characteristics such as hair or eye color on or off.

THE COMPUTER CHIP

First created to shrink electronics so they could fit into nuclear warheads, computer chips have had an impact on the modern world that is out of all proportion to their tiny size.

THE DIGITAL AGE began not with silicon chips but with valves. As the switches and amplifiers in the first electronic computers, valves worked like miniature light bulbs and glowed just as hot. Finding a smaller replacement became an obsession for the electronics companies of the 1940s, as it would make possible miniature circuits—and simple computers—that generated less heat.

FIRST TRANSISTORS

The first to succeed were Americans John Bardeen and Walter Brattain. In December 1947, they wrapped a triangle of plastic in gold foil and pressed it against a chunk of the metal-like element germanium. This is a semiconductor: it can be coaxed into either blocking an electrical current, as glass does, or conducting it, like a copper wire. Bardeen and Brattain's device was an untidy mess of wires, but it was a working transistor: a simple amplifier. Transistors gradually replaced valves, and by 1954, radios—which had previously been pieces of furniture—had shrunk to pocket size.

NOBODY NEEDS A COMPUTER
The world was slow to wake up to the power and potential of computers. Even those who were closely involved with their creation were skeptical. In 1953, the head of IBM, Thomas J. Watson, suggested that his company expected to sell just five computers in the United States.

INTEGRATED CIRCUITS

Transistors were tiny, but they still weren't small enough. The United States and the Soviet Union were threatening each other with nuclear missiles in the Cold War—a tense rivalry that stopped short of actual fighting. To fit inside missile warheads, guidance computers needed to be tiny. By the spring of 1959, two more U.S. researchers had independently come up with a way to cram transistors into ever smaller spaces. Teams led by Robert Noyce of Fairchild Semiconductor and Jack Kilby of Texas Instruments both managed to squeeze several components onto a chip of semiconductor. Their integrated circuits (ICs) shrank the computer of a Minuteman missile by three quarters and cut the number of separate transistors by nearly 7,000.

> ## "I don't have any recollection of a 'Boom! There it is!' light bulb going off."
>
> **ROBERT NOYCE, INVENTOR OF THE INTEGRATED CIRCUIT, ON THE MOMENT HE HAD THE IDEA, 1982**

ICs quickly spread from missiles to civilian computers, and chips replaced more and more individual components. Jack Kilby's chip incorporated just one transistor, a capacitor, and three resistors. The first personal computers, built in 1974, used a chip that had 6,000 transistors. Today's chips incorporate billions and have revolutionized every aspect of our lives. Cell phones represent the pinnacle of miniaturization: if your phone used 1940s valves instead of silicon chips, it would be the size of a small city and would soak up the current from two nuclear power stations to make a single call.

COSTLY COMPUTERS
In the 1960s, an IBM computer took up a whole floor of an air-conditioned office and cost several million dollars. By 1980, you could buy a personal computer with similar power for $1,500.

INTEGRATED CIRCUITS

Integrated circuits (ICs) are crystals of silicon printed with microscopic patterns, which are etched and infused with impurities such as phosphorus. This process can create many different kinds of devices on the chip. The four most common are transistors, diodes, resistors, and capacitors. Each component is represented by a special symbol on a circuit diagram.

TRANSISTOR

The most important device on a chip, a transistor can switch a signal or amplify it, i.e., make it stronger.

DIODE

Working like a water valve, a diode allows current to pass in one direction but blocks it from flowing the other way.

RESISTOR

Perhaps the simplest of all devices on a chip is the resistor, which reduces the flow of current in a circuit.

CAPACITOR

By storing electrical charge, a capacitor can work as a tiny power source or as a filter, and do many other jobs.

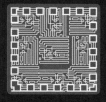
IC

The IC is put in a plastic pack to make it easier to handle.

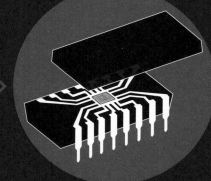

ICs are soldered onto a circuit board. Copper lines connect pins to the chips.

MOORE'S LAW
Robert Noyce's boss at Fairchild Semiconductor was Gordon Moore, who famously predicted in 1965 that for 10 years the number of components on silicon chips would double every year. He was right, and the growth continued: since 1975, chip performance has doubled roughly every two years.

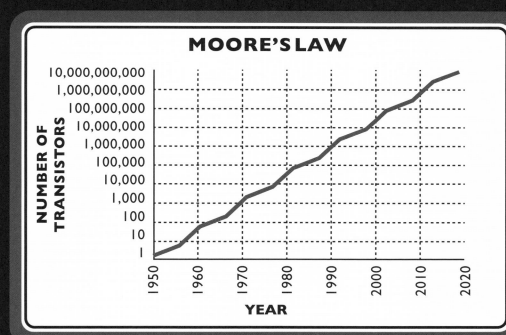

MOORE'S LAW

NUMBER OF TRANSISTORS

10,000,000,000
1,000,000,000
100,000,000
10,000,000
1,000,000
100,000
10,000
1,000
100
10
1

1950 1960 1970 1980 1990 2000 2010 2020

YEAR

Smaller electronic devices such as laptops have a single circuit board.

SPACE EXPLORATION

Reaching for the stars stretched 1960s technology and resources to the limits—but not as much as it stretched our minds and our sense of our place in the cosmos.

SENDING HUMANS TO EXPLORE space is difficult, costly, and inefficient. Keeping them alive, safe, and sane in space requires heavy, complex systems and supplies. Robotic explorers suffer none of these disadvantages, but uncrewed missions don't make news headlines in the same way as human space explorers: unlike astronauts, robots cannot be brave.

DANGER AND DISCOMFORT

Courage was a quality that the first space explorers possessed in abundance, as is made painfully clear when you look at their capsules in a museum. *Freedom 7*, the craft of America's first astronaut, Alan Shepard, is tiny and crude. No wider than a man's height, it has an instrument panel made up mostly of simple switches, and it lacks computers of any kind. The outside is still charred and streaked from the furnace heat of reentry, and just a few centimeters of insulation protected the astronaut from rapid cremation.

"I CAN'T WAIT!"
Technical hitches delayed the launch of *Freedom 7*, and during the three-hour wait, Alan Shepard became desperate to pee. Since the flight was scheduled to last just 15 minutes, engineers had not planned for this. Rather than clamber out and further delay launch, he peed in his space suit.

SPACE RACE

Shepard's May 1961 mission made him a patriotic hero: not only was he the first American to defy gravity and (almost) go into orbit, he was also a pioneer in what had become known as the "space race." America's foe, the Soviet Union, had launched the first satellite, *Sputnik*, some four years earlier (see page 52), kicking off more than a decade of rivalry in which the two nations fought to launch the most ambitious and sophisticated capsules and space probes.

The space race became a race to the moon, which the United States won in 1969, when *Apollo 11* landed on the lunar surface. This great achievement, to which 400,000 people contributed, was undeniably spectacular, but what did it really achieve for those of us who gazed enviously upward from Earth? In fact, space research led to many

BAILING OUT
On April 12, 1961, Yuri Gagarin became the first person to travel into space. As his capsule returned to Earth, he ejected and descended the last 4 miles (7 kilometers) by parachute. This was kept secret for 10 years because the rules of the spaceflight governing body Fédération Aéronautique Internationale stated that astronauts must land with their craft.

advances great and small, including solar panels, water purification, and tiny computers. But these improvements are trivial when compared to the dramatic change it wrought in how we see ourselves. From the viewpoint of a spaceship bound for the moon, Earth is a small, fragile blue blob. Photographs of it floating in the deep black of space made us cherish our planet as never before and take the first faltering steps toward protecting it for future generations.

ULTIMATE TOURIST JOYRIDE
Space exploration isn't just for professional astronauts: tourists are joining them in orbit. Seven joyriders each paid millions to visit the International Space Station, and several hundred would-be passengers booked tickets when Virgin Galactic announced plans for suborbital flights.

"Fix your little problem and light this candle!"
ASTRONAUT ALAN SHEPARD URGES MISSION CONTROL TO LAUNCH THE REDSTONE ROCKET THAT WILL CARRY HIM INTO SPACE IN MAY 1961

MULTISTAGE ROCKET SYSTEM

Most space launches use several "stages," each with separate engines and fuel supplies. Each stage is smaller and lighter than the last, so by discarding spent stages, the rocket carries the least weight into space. The vast Saturn V rocket that launched the missions of Apollo, the U.S. human spaceflight program, had three stages and could lift into orbit craft weighing up to 260,000 pounds (118,000 kilograms).

First stage
The biggest of the three stages, the first stage burned through more than 4.4 million pounds (2 million kilograms) of liquid fuel and oxygen in less than three minutes. In that time, it lifted each Apollo spacecraft to an altitude of 42 miles (68 kilometers). Once spent, the first stage dropped away and fell back to Earth.

Second stage
The second stage carried the Apollo craft through the upper atmosphere. When its fuel was exhausted, after about six minutes, this stage separated and fell back to Earth. The engines on the third stage then fired.

Third stage
Only the third stage reached Earth's orbit. The three Apollo modules sat at the top of this stage. Below were rocket engines and fuel tanks, which were discarded after the trip to the moon began.

APOLLO SPACECRAFT
The National Aeronautics and Space Administration (NASA) flew astronauts to the moon in six successful Apollo missions between 1969 and 1972. Each Apollo spacecraft had three parts. The command module — the main crew capsule — remained attached to the service module in lunar orbit while the lunar module descended to the moon's surface. Command and service modules returned from the moon, but only the command module reentered Earth's atmosphere.

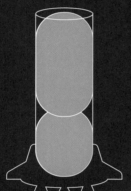

Once en route to the moon, the crew performed a delicate maneuver and then discarded the empty third-stage fuel tanks and engines.

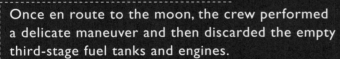

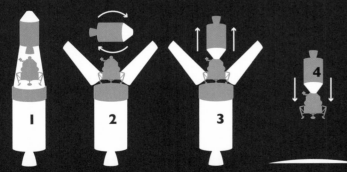

1. The three Apollo modules reach Earth's orbit.
2. The command and service modules (CSM) separate and turn.
3. The CSM dock with, and extract, the lunar module.
4. The CSM and lunar modules journey to the moon together.

COMMAND MODULE

Each three-person Apollo crew spent between 6 and 12 days living in a space no bigger than five fridges.

SERVICE MODULE

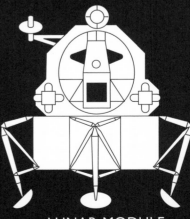

LUNAR MODULE

THE INTERNET

Vast, sophisticated, and now essential, the internet was crudely bolted together by U.S. war generals, San Francisco hippies, and an engineer at CERN, Europe's giant atom smasher.

THE IDEA OF THE INTERNET—a network of networks—began in 1960 as a way to link United States radar warning stations and missile launch sites. Defense chiefs feared that military phone lines used to issue orders were vulnerable: an enemy missile strike could cut them, preventing a revenge attack. Researcher Paul Baran found a way to ensure that signals would always get through. They were chopped into tiny "packets" that could find their own way around a network, which meant that the order to strike back could bypass destroyed cables.

THE INTERNET BEGINS

Baran's idea was so novel that it was rejected, but by 1969, the Advanced Research Projects Agency had begun to link military computing centers in a network called ARPANET. More networks followed over the next 20 years, allowing universities to share information and computing power. Connections between these networks created the internet.

Although private and business users began to go online in 1989, there was hardly a stampede to connect. To perform even simple tasks, users had to type long, obscure commands and wait patiently. Nevertheless, a few online communities flourished. In San Francisco, the WELL (Whole Earth 'Lectronic Link) was run by former hippies. Their value of freedom and their opposition to control strongly influenced internet culture and are still evident in resources such as Wikipedia.

"In a few years, men will be able to communicate more effectively through a machine than face-to-face."

ROBERT TAYLOR AND J. C. R. LICKLIDER, PIONEERS OF ARPANET, FORESEE THE INTERNET IN 1968

INVENTING EMAIL
In 1971, engineer Ray Tomlinson created the email system we know today by suggesting the use of the @ symbol to separate the names of users from the network they worked on. He modestly shrugged off the idea as "a no-brainer."

BIRTH OF THE WEB

The internet might have remained a system for academics and geeks if it hadn't been for British computer scientist Tim Berners-Lee. Working at European nuclear research organization CERN, he wanted to find a way for researchers to share their work. He suggested marking up text to highlight words that linked to other, connected pages. His "Hypertext Markup Language," or HTML, was to become the vocabulary of the web. Berners-Lee's "WorldWideWeb" browser was at first too simple to show anything but text, but that changed in 1993 with the development of Mosaic, which could also display images. Though crude and slow, Mosaic was (just) recognizable as the familiar web of today.

Since 1993, the internet has come to mean much more than the web and email. Connected to the remotest places by undersea cables and satellite links (see opposite), it keeps our world running. Without it, supermarket shelves would be empty and roads gridlocked. In our personal lives we rely on it for everything from finding true love to keeping up with distant friends. And it is our main way of getting news and entertainment. Not bad for a system that was once dismissed as "too complicated" to work.

SMILE!
The smiley face was in use on the internet long before it became the standard SMS signal for a joke. Scott Fahlman, a U.S. computer scientist, suggested using it in 1982 after his fellow workers mistakenly took a joke about a mercury spill seriously.

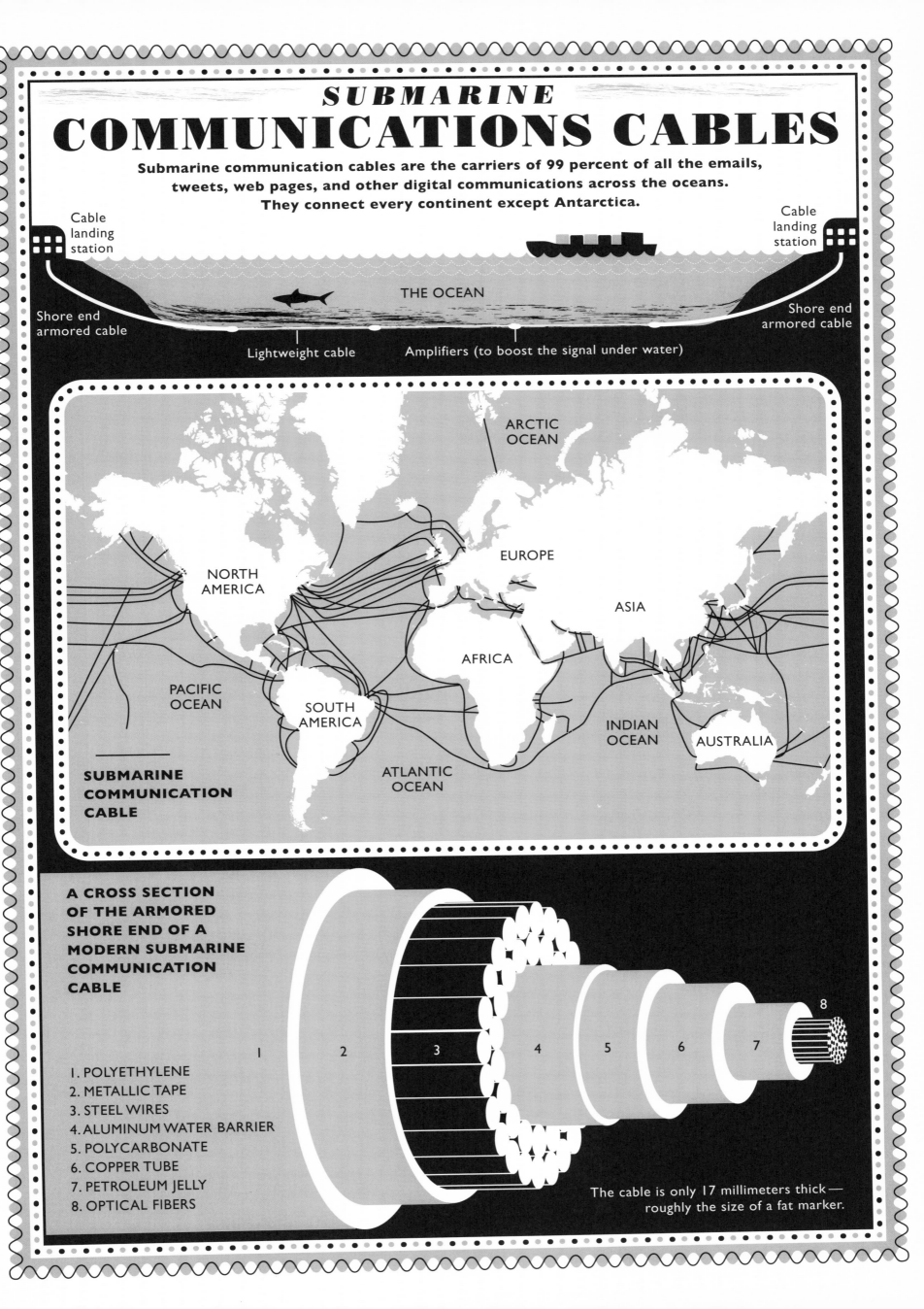

SUBMARINE
COMMUNICATIONS CABLES

Submarine communication cables are the carriers of 99 percent of all the emails, tweets, web pages, and other digital communications across the oceans. They connect every continent except Antarctica.

Cable landing station

Cable landing station

Shore end armored cable

Shore end armored cable

THE OCEAN

Lightweight cable

Amplifiers (to boost the signal under water)

ARCTIC OCEAN

EUROPE

NORTH AMERICA

ASIA

AFRICA

PACIFIC OCEAN

SOUTH AMERICA

INDIAN OCEAN

AUSTRALIA

ATLANTIC OCEAN

SUBMARINE COMMUNICATION CABLE

A CROSS SECTION OF THE ARMORED SHORE END OF A MODERN SUBMARINE COMMUNICATION CABLE

1. POLYETHYLENE
2. METALLIC TAPE
3. STEEL WIRES
4. ALUMINUM WATER BARRIER
5. POLYCARBONATE
6. COPPER TUBE
7. PETROLEUM JELLY
8. OPTICAL FIBERS

The cable is only 17 millimeters thick—roughly the size of a fat marker.

ARTIFICIAL INTELLIGENCE

As computers increase in power, they are learning skills we once considered uniquely human. This artificial intelligence can improve our lives . . . provided society shares the benefits fairly.

A LTHOUGH COMPUTERS have been referred to as "electronic brains" since their invention, making them actually learn and think is a recent innovation. Creating the illusion of artificial intelligence (AI) wasn't difficult: as early as 1957, programmers had built a computer chess program that could beat an average human.

SLOW PROGRESS

Going further proved slow and difficult, but by the 1980s, computers were capable of hosting expert systems—reasoning programs that could make decisions based on set rules. Early expert systems became useful aids in medical diagnosis, and gradually AI made progress in other fields: computers were taught to read printed text, and to both speak and recognize speech. As number-crunching power mushroomed, programmers found new ways to solve old problems. For example, machine translation was impossible as long as researchers tried to make computers understand text. But when they were fed billions of documents in many languages, computers used brute force to translate. Once they had learned which words corresponded in each language pair, they become passable interpreters.

SUPER-INTELLIGENT MACHINES?
The terrifying prospect that computers and robots might one day become more intelligent than their makers, and endanger them, has long inspired writers and filmmakers. In 1942, science-fiction writer Isaac Asimov proposed laws to ensure that robots are obedient and do not harm humans.

CHANGING OUR WORLD

Today, the most advanced AI systems don't need teaching. Through "reinforcement learning"—a form of trial and error—they evolve strategies to help them succeed at a task. In 2017, tech giant Google unveiled an AI program that played the ancient Chinese game of Go, called AlphaGo. The AI was taught only the basic rules, and in three days

> ## "Machines will be capable, within twenty years, of doing any work a man can do."
>
> **FROM HERBERT SIMON'S *THE SHAPE OF AUTOMATION FOR MEN AND MANAGEMENT*, 1965**

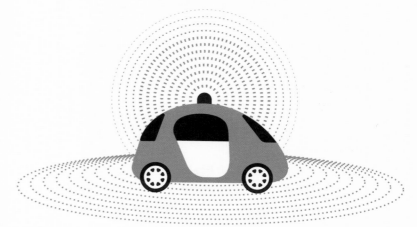

CHEATING AI
AI has to be smart enough to know when to bend the rules. When early self-driving cars reached intersections, they waited obediently as the law demands, but the passing traffic never slowed. Engineers had to tweak the software to make the cars inch slowly forward—just as human drivers do—until drivers on the main road gave way.

it had become an expert player. After 40 days' practice it beat the world champion.

AI has advanced so far and so fast that we now take it for granted. We have ceased to marvel at a robot answering the phone, and just get irritated at how long we have to talk to it before reaching a human. AI powers the most sophisticated emerging technologies. It guides the autonomous vehicles that will soon revolutionize transportation, giving new mobility to those who can't drive. It is eliminating the dullest office tasks and giving robots humanlike skills to do dangerous, dirty jobs. If we can find new, rewarding roles for the drivers, cashiers, and manual workers whom AI will replace, this astonishing technology has the potential to free us from mind-numbing labor and give us all wealthier, healthier lives.

Many individual brain functions take place in specific regions, but our brains are amazingly adaptable. If injury destroys a specialized area, other areas may take over the lost skills.

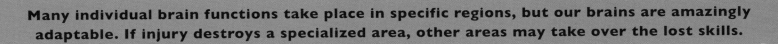

SENSORY CORTEX
Receives sensations from the body

PARIETAL LOBE
Processes language and senses

TEMPORAL LOBE
Processes and remembers sensations

OCCIPITAL LOBE
Processes visual information

WERNICKE'S AREA
Controls language understanding

CEREBELLUM
Controls movement, attention, and language

BRAIN STEM
Controls breathing, heartbeat, and other involuntary functions

MOTOR CORTEX
Controls movement

FRONTAL LOBE
Controls reasoning and judgment

BROCA'S AREA
Controls speech production

OLFACTORY BULB
Controls sense of smell

LIMBIC SYSTEM
Controls emotions, behavior, and memory

Weighing about 3 pounds (1.4 kilograms), the human brain has the wobbly texture of Jell-O. It is a hungry organ, consuming up to one-fifth of our energy.

The spinal cord carries nerves from the brain stem down to the body's limbs and organs.

Though the brain works by sending electrical impulses along nerves, at one-tenth of a volt, these are very weak. A flashlight battery is 20 times stronger.

MAN VS. MACHINE

Comparing a computer to the human brain reveals some striking similarities — but the differences between hardware and "wetware" are equally compelling.

SIMILARITIES

Just as brains receive and process input from our senses and memory, computers receive data and process it systematically to produce a useful result.

The computer's transistors are like the brain's 100 billion neurons. But the biggest CPUs (central processing units) currently have only a fifth of this number of transistors.

Brains and computers both need a power supply. Electricity keeps a computer running, and our brains rely on the oxygen and sugars carried in our blood.

There are many ways to compare brain and computer, but the most significant point of comparison is the potential for growth. Our brain-power cannot expand beyond our skulls, but computers get faster daily — and may eventually grow smarter than we are.

DIFFERENCES

Though AI software (see left) teaches computers to learn, even the most complex cannot compete with the learning ability of a toddler's brain.

Despite what you see in movies, computers are not conscious: our brains make us aware of ourselves and our surroundings.

In computers, hardware and software are completely separate. But in the human brain, neurons both process information and store it as memories.

To Mum
J. B.

*To all the team at Walker, who have worked
so hard to make this a great book*
R. P.

The following people generously gave their time to help the author and editors check facts and confirm details:
Michael Chazan, Mary Fissell, Tom Jackson, Ron Lancaster, and Emeline Pasquier

First U.S. edition 2019

Library of Congress Catalog Card Number 2019939179
ISBN 978-1-5362-0766-8

19 20 21 22 23 24 LEO 10 9 8 7 6 5 4 3 2 1

Printed in Heshan, Guangdong, China

This book was typeset in Gill and Bodoni.
The illustrations were screen-printed.

Candlewick Studio
an imprint of
Candlewick Press
99 Dover Street
Somerville, Massachusetts 02144

www.candlewickstudio.com